M000199654

OUT OF EGYPT INTO CANAAN

Lessons in Spiritual Geography

by
MARTIN WELLS KNAPP

Editor of
"The Revivalist"
and
Author of
Impressions

"For whatsoever things were written
aforetime were written for our learning, that we through
patience and comfort of the Scriptures might have
hope."—Romans 15:4.

SCHMUL PUBLISHING CO.
SCHMUL'S WESLEYAN BOOK CLUB   SALEM, OHIO

COPYRIGHT © 2000 BY SCHMUL PUBLISHING CO.
All rights reserved. No part of this publication may be reproduced or used in any form or by any means—graphic, electronic, or mechanical, including photocopying, recording, taping, or information storage or retrieval systems—without prior written permission of the publishers.

Published by Schmul Publishing Co.
PO Box 716
Salem, Ohio USA

Printed in the United States of America

Printed by Old Paths Tract Society
RR2, Box 43
Shoals, Indiana 47581

ISBN 0-88019-412-X

Contents

With Congratulations

to

GOD'S BIBLE SCHOOL, COLLEGE
AND

MISSIONARY TRAINING HOME

For a Century of Holiness Education and Leadership.

May you ever fulfill the vision of your Founder

MARTIN WELLS KNAPP

*in providing quality, Bible-centered education for students
of holy living.*

—The Publishers—

UNTO THE
"FATHER OF OUR LORD JESUS CHRIST,
of whom the whole family
in heaven and earth is named;"
who gave His Son for our redemption,
and His Spirit for our regeneration,
cleansing, and enduement;

BY WHOSE GRACE AND COUNSELS

this book has been written,
and who alone is able to effectually
apply its truths, and overrule any mistakes
that may be therein to his glory:
and unto his blood-bought ones,
who still are in spiritual bondage,
and the great family of
His beloved children, — this

SIMPLE ILLUSTRATIVE STORY

Of the Way
OUT OF EGYPT'S DARKNESS
INTO THE CANAAN LAND
of joyful service,
by one of the least of his children is humbly

DEDICATED.

Foreword

THROUGHOUT THE SUMMER OF 1900, Martin Wells Knapp (1853-1901) unveiled his plan for a new Bible School and Missionary Training Home in the pages of *The Revivalist,* which he had edited since its inception in 1888. A renowned holiness evangelist, Knapp had risen from relative obscurity as a backwoods Methodist pastor to command the attention of a vast army of holiness people coalesced under his leadership to form a dynamic spiritual force, the Revivalist Movement. By 1900, it was very likely that he was the most influential man in the American Holiness Movement, with *The Revivalist* surpassing a circulation of 25,000.

Knapp had suffered with various physical ailments since his youth. This undoubtedly reinforced his desire that the forces unleashed in the Revivalist Movement be perpetuated long after his demise. To this end, he proposed establishing a school dedicated to—in fact, owned by— God, to be superintended by Knapp until "in case of death or incapacity" it would pass into the hands of his "successor or successors, whoever they may be."[1] He thus wrote, "We anticipate that the proposed Bible-school and Missionary Training-home will be largely a continuation of the work we are now engaged in."[2]

A primary concern for Knapp was that most Christian education, even that under Wesleyan auspices, had become enamored with secular subjects and had relegated study of the Scriptures to the periphery of college programs. He lamented, "The ignorance of Christians, and even of ministers of the gospel, of the Word of God is simply appalling; and it is due largely to our system of training." With the motto, "Back to the Bible," he determined to help remedy this at God's Bible School by making it an institution "where the Bible will be the main book studied, other books being studied only as aids to the mastery of this—a school where it will be honored as the great Mississippi River of research and spiritual culture, into which all others are but tributary streams."[3]

Elaborating on his burden for Bible-centered education, Knapp asserted that a Christian should be as familiar with the Bible as with the multiplication tables. He observed that "the most proficient mathematician is as powerless as a babe to work out the simplest problems in spiritual loss and gain." He further asserted that one may have an excellent grasp of geography, "and yet be totally ignorant of the location of spiritual Canaan."[4] It was to prepare Christian workers adept in explaining this spiritual geography to seeking souls that God's Bible School was founded.

A similar purpose had incited Knapp several years earlier (1887) to write a book explaining holiness concepts in terms of spiritual geography, *Out of Egypt into Canaan*.[5] Interpreting the history of ancient Israel, particularly the Exodus and Conquest, as symbolic of holiness experience, Knapp used Canaan language to describe spiritual progress from conversion to glorification, especially focusing on entire sanctification. The resultant work, reminiscent of John Bunyan's *Pilgrim's Progress*, remains a holiness classic, perhaps the best book-length example of holiness typological Bible interpretation.

God's Bible School has continued to perpetuate holiness teachings for a century now, aiding many on their journey from Egypt to Canaan and preparing thousands of students to share their knowledge of spiritual geography with others. Knapp's dream has been realized. However, his book which so lucidly sets forth his holiness exposition in Canaan language has become quite rare, a prize for collectors. It is thus indeed a fitting tribute that this publisher is again making this primary work by Martin Wells Knapp available in conjunction with the centenary of God's Bible School and Missionary Training Home.

—Wallace Thornton, Jr.
Author, *Radical Righteousness:
Personal Ethics and the Development of the Holiness Movement* (1998)
and *Back to the Bible: The Story of
God's Bible School* (forthcoming)

Endnotes

1. "In Trust for God," *The Revivalist*, (June 21, 1900), 5.

2. "The Work Continued," *The Revivalist* (June 21, 1900), 5.

3. "Deplorable Ignorance," *The Revivalist* (June 21, 1900), 2.

4. "Chaff and Wheat," *The Revivalist* (June 28, 1900), 1.

5. Although copyrighted in 1887, the book was not published until the following year.

OUT OF EGYPT INTO CANAAN

"Out of Darkness into His Marvelous Light"

Where are you?

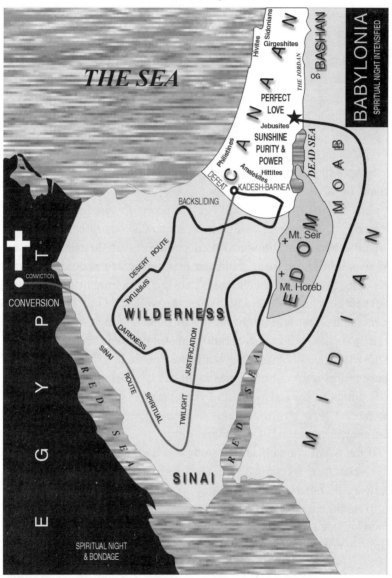

This map is designed to show the routes of Israel and spiritual states illustrated by events occurring in them. It should be carefully studied in connection with the reading of the book.

Preface

THE AUTHOR'S OBJECT IN writing this book is to glorify God by riveting the reader's attention to some of the great spiritual truths so vividly illustrated by the history of Israel during the period under consideration. The line of thought here pursued has been helpful to him and those to whom it has been orally presented, and he trusts it may be still more richly blessed in this form.

Scriptural warrant for seeking practical lessons in this way may be found in many places. Referring to these truths, "it is written" in Psalms 78:5-8, "For he established a testimony in Jacob, and appointed a law in Israel, which he commanded our fathers that they should make them known to their children: that the generation to come might know them, even the children which should be born; who should arise and declare them unto their children: that they might set their hope in God, and not forget the works of God, but keep his commandments: and might not be as their fathers, a stubborn and rebellious generation, a generation that set not their heart aright, and whose spirit was not steadfast with God." Also, in 1 Cor. 10: 6, "Now these things were our examples to the intent we should not lust after evil things as they also lusted." And verse 11 of the same chapter declares: "Now all these things happened unto them for examples, and they are written for our admonition."

If the writer can help any to study and heed the tragical and heroic ensamples there recorded he will feel that he has not written in vain. He is aware that others have written ably upon this subject, and is not so vain as to suppose he can excel them, but writes to exercise that "power for good" alluded to by the saintly and venerable Bishop Janes when he said, "Every man has his circle of influence; each author on this subject will secure some readers that would not give attention to the writings of others. Here is a power for good that ought not to be lost."

It is humbly hoped that this book may be like a lamp, and the truths herein like the light from it, and that the reader will be so charmed by the radiance of the light that any defects in the lamp may thus be in a measure atoned for.

That the light may lead into the rich experience of which the earthly Canaan is the type is the author's sincere prayer.

—M. W. Knapp

Albion, Michigan

1

In Egypt: Spiritual Bondage

Prelude

WHEREFORE SAY UNTO THE children of Israel, I am the Lord, and I will bring you out from under the burdens of the Egyptians, and I will rid you out of their bondage, and I will redeem you with a stretched out arm and great judgments, and I will take you to me for a people, and I will be your God who bringeth you out from under the burdens of the Egyptians. And I will bring you in unto the land which I did swear to give to Abraham, to Isaac and to Jacob, and I will give it to you for an heritage; I am the LORD. — Exodus 6:6-8.

That he would grant unto us, that we, being delivered out of the hand of our enemies, might serve him without fear, in holiness and righteousness before him, all the days of our life.
—Luke 1:74, 75

> *When in error's chains we groaned,*
> *Jesus for our sins atoned;*
> *Purchased pardon for the race,*
> *Offered free and boundless grace.*
> *See! in might he now appears,*
> *Breaks our chains, dispels our fears.*

In Egypt: Spiritual Bondage

EGYPT, THE LAND WHERE Israel was kept captive, is illustrative of the kingdom of darkness, wherein all of the unconverted are enslaved.

Pharaoh, the name of Egypt's kings, is illustrative of Satan, who leads the impenitent captive at his will.

Israel is illustrative of the soul as it passes from the bondage of sin into the liberty of the Son.

The events at the Red Sea are illustrative of those which occur at the conversion of the soul.

Events between the Red Sea and Kadesh Barnea in the "Sinai Wilderness" experience are illustrative of those in the true believer's life from the time of conversion until he "receives the fullness of the Holy Ghost."

Kadesh Barnea, the place where Israel was defeated as upon the very verge of victory, illustrates the defeat of many who were just about to receive the fullness of divine love.

The Wilderness, where Israel wandered forty years and all of the disobedient perished, illustrates the life of the backslider, or the man who knows his duty and will not do it.

Events at the Jordan are illustrative of those that occur at the time of entire sanctification.

Canaan is illustrative of union with Christ on earth.

Babylon is illustrative of the lives of those who have fallen from spiritual Canaan.

Israel enslaved is the sad picture which first greets our vision. Though this people had been chosen by God for his "peculiar treasure," we find them the slaves of hard masters Just so with unsaved man: he was created for companionship with his Maker, but he is found in bondage more cruel than that of Pharaoh; for Jesus said, "Whosoever committeth sin is the servant of sin."

In this slavery there was apparent prosperity. "The children of Israel were fruitful and increased abundantly." (Ex. 1:3.) So the wicked sometimes prosper marvelously; buy, sell, and get gain; pull down their buildings and build greater; clothe themselves in purple and fine linen; fare sumptuously every day, and, for getting their Maker and his claims upon them, say, "We are happy now, and have neither time nor inclination to think about the future; let that take care for itself." At the same time they are away from their Father's house, subject to the government of sin, and in the power of Satan.

Their prosperity was limited. "There arose a new king, that knew not Joseph." (Ex. 1:8.) He "set over them taskmasters to afflict them with their burdens." This is a graphic picture of the sinner's joy. "In prosperity the destroyer cometh upon him," and "suddenly he shall be cut off." "When he shall say peace and safety, then sudden destruction cometh upon him."

Pharaoh put the best first. So with Satan. With him it is first the sparkling wine, then the tasteless compound, and at the last invariably the bitter dregs. He says, "Sow the wild oats," have "a good time," "cut your mother's apron strings," "glory in your freedom," and soon when you are racked with pain, the results of these excesses, or buried in the shame which they have brought, he laughs at your misery.

Their service proved hard indeed. "They made their lives bitter with hard bondage ... all their service wherewith they made them serve was with rigor." (Ex. 1:14.) "The way of the transgressor is hard." It is "full of misery," and the way of peace and life is far from it. The poisonous bait which Satan offers in the many forms of sensual indulgence and worldly pride and pleasures may taste sweet for the moment, but soon it is followed by spiritual convulsions, that without a divine remedy must end in death eternal. However deceptively delightful this bondage may be at first, ere it ends it lashes both soul and body with more than scorpion strokes.

Israel was offered deliverance. Divinely chosen and divinely protected, Moses appeared to set them free. So Jesus was "chosen" and raised up for the spiritual emancipation of all who will believe upon him. "Whom the Son makes free is free indeed."

Deliverance was provided for every captive. So with the great Gospel deliverance. The Savior will save unto the uttermost all that come unto God by him.

Israel at first rejected deliverance. "Who made thee a prince and a judge over us?" was the angry question they hurled into the face of their God-sent deliverer on his first appearance. It was not until after years more of bitter bondage that they yielded to God's herald of freedom. Precisely so it is with many to whom the Savior offers freedom and life. At first they are indifferent, and perhaps insolent. Time passes, and health fails, pleasures lose their charms, earthly ambitions burst like bubbles, wealth takes wings, friends forsake, loved ones are laid in the grave, death is at the door, or some other kindred calamity threatens; and then the heart, harrowed by sorrow, is ready to receive that deliverance that, if accepted at first, would have saved untold bitterness.

I knew a self-willed man who said proudly: "I'll not yield now." Shortly the family circle was broken by a bolt of lightning, and his heart was softened. "I have lost a fortune," said one who had been a merchant prince, "but, thank God, it has led me to receive a kingdom." It was not until John B. Gough reached the awful experience which he describes as follows that he was ready to forsake the Egypt of sin and accept the Savior's proffered aid. He said,

> I turned to my work brokenhearted, crushed in spirit and paralyzed in energy, feeling how low I had sunk in the esteem of prudent and sober-minded men. Suddenly the small bar I held in my hand began to move; I felt it move; I griped it; still it moved and twisted; I gripped it still harder, yet the thing would move until I could feel it—yes, *feel* it—tearing the palm out of my hand; there I dropped it, and there it lay, a curling, slimy snake! I could hear the paper shavings rustle as the horrible thing writhed before me! If it *had been* a snake I should not have minded it; I was never afraid of a snake; I should have called someone to have looked at it; I could have killed it. I should not have been terrified at a *thing*, but I knew it was a dead, cold, bar of iron, and there it was with its green eyes, its forked, darting tongue, curling in all its slimy loathsomeness, and the horror filled me so that my hair seemed to stand up and shiver, and my skin lift from the scalp to the ankles, and I groaned out, "I cannot fight this through! O my God! I shall die! I cannot fight it!" It was only after such struggles as this that he was willing to accept Christ's great deliverance.

Sorrow, sickness, bereavements, and like judgments are the only agencies that will awaken some from the sleep of sin.

Father, let such influences come rather than precious souls should be lost forever.

One king, but many taskmasters. Pharaoh was the one king to whose power they were subject, but he placed over them many taskmasters, with orders to make them serve with "rigor." The sinner has one master, and he is Satan. Over the souls of his subjects on earth he has appointed two general overseers. The name of one is "The World," of the other, "The Flesh." The three constitute the trinity of hell. Under the two are several iron-hearted taskmasters, with deceptive tongues and scorpion whips with which to lash the soul to labor. They are all gory with the blood of souls they have slaughtered for their master. A few of them will be noticed by name.

Drunkenness. His victims are first lured by the seemingly harmless glass, which often is resented by the hand of some fair enchantress. He says, "Take a little; it will brace you up and do you good;" "You can cease any time you will." His victim listens, quaffs the cup, and wildly dreams that he is free and happy. Soon he says, "I'll stop." He tries to. He fails. He tries again, with like results. The silken strands have become iron cables, and almost frenzied he awakes to the awful fact that he is a slave to drink. Listen to his testimony:

> Horrible faces glared upon me from the walls—faces ever changing and displaying new and still more horrible features; black, bloated insects crawled over my face, and myriads of burning concentric rings were revolving incessantly. I seemed to have a knife with hundreds of blades in my hand, every blade driven through the flesh, and all so inextricably bent and tangled together that I could not withdraw them for some time, and when I did, from my lacerated fingers the bloody fibers would stretch out all quivering with pain.

Such struggles between Drunkenness and his slaves could be counted by the thousand every day. He has no mercy, and counts his victims by the thousand in every quarter of the globe.

Licentiousness. This soul-enslaving demon is no less deceptive and merciless than his brother just mentioned. He allures into his service at first by promises of pleasures enticingly attractive. Such they seem for a season, and then begin to fade, and soon the slave to lust finds power to enjoy it gone, and also the power to resist the temptation to indulgence has been lost. Now the keen lashes of his taskmaster's whip begin to play with cruel fury. Disgraced and ruined in soul and body, his steps even here take hold of hell.

Mammon. More subtle and deceptive in his approaches than either of the others and just as cruel in his final mastery of the soul is mammon, god of money. He whispers to the soul: "Get earthly gain;" "Lay up treasure for yourself below." As riches increase he gives a temporary satisfaction that sometimes is taken for real enjoyment. Soon this gives place to fear of failure, corroding care, fear of robbery, and dread of death that any instant may separate from earthly gain forever. Now "business drives him;" there is "no time" for social converse with his family, for prayer at the home altar, for studying the "chart of life," or worship on God's holy day. Now under the crack of his master mammon's whip, he continues to toil and worry. His bondage is bitter. No rest, no respite, no Sabbath; he is a slave seven days every week and twenty-four hours every day, for his sleep is full of dreams of hurried toil. A wealthy lumber merchant said to me when questioned in regard to preparation for eternity: "I have never had time to think about it." Awful slavery!

Selfish Ambition. He, too, has thousands beneath his cutting lash. They toil and study and plan for the exaltation of self and selfish interests. It may be that for a time they exult in success; but soon their gilded bubbles begin to burst, and then follows bitter disappointment and perhaps a lifetime of futile effort to retrieve the past. We say sometimes that they "die from disappointment." They live slaves, and die slaves, and merciless ambition is their taskmaster.

Fashion. "Fashion" is the Jezebel of all the ages. A more exacting oppressor earth never knew. To be able to dress so as to move in certain circles, a woman in one of our cities actually deprived her children of food and fuel, and thus caused their death. To meet the demands of this heartless wretch, thousands have sacrificed time, means, honor, virtue, and life itself. Her laws are as heartless and stringent as the iron codes of the ancients. President Finney tells of a fashionable woman, who, when approached on the subject of immediate decision for Christ, "wept and confessed that this had been her snare; and she was afraid that her love of dress and society would ruin her soul. She confessed that she had been neglecting the salvation of her soul because she did not know how to break away from the circle in which she moved."

Tobacco. This taskmaster is a devil indeed, and a black one at that. A Church member told me last Spring that he would give $500 to be free from his bondage. He is twin brother to alcohol. Stinginess, peevishness, and filthiness delight to call him father. He often whips his slaves until they "feel too poor" to take a religious paper, and cannot afford to pay much to spread the Gospel. At the same time they will squander dollars every year in his service. He blackens the teeth, pollutes the breath, deranges the stomach, and benumbs the brain. When his victims see their slavery and attempt to assert freedom, like Israel's masters, he increases their burdens, and will not "let them go." With the scorpion whip of cancers, heart disease, and kindred maladies, he has finally whipped many of his unhappy victims to death, and then laughed at their dying throes.

Opium, hasheesh, and several other taskmasters from the families of stimulants and narcotics, ply the lash over millions more of pitiable victims.

Pride, public opinion, and passion have scourged to the death countless multitudes and hold in chains today millions more who never drew the breath of spiritual freedom.

Other masters might be mentioned, but enough have been to show that the souls enslaved, like Israel's, have been many.

Pharaoh represented Moses' message as delusive. "Let them not regard vain words," was his ironical command. A like spirit has been manifested by Satan and his ranks of God and man haters in all ages. They have ever called God's messengers "fools," "lunatics," and "fanatics," and scoffed at their messages as "idle tales." They are ever ready to whisper to the awakened and inquiring sinner, "You have too much to give up," "You will lose in your business," "You will forfeit your friends," "You cannot break off old habits," "You cannot hold out," and thousands of like suggestions, that give the lie to Christ's promises of profit in both this and the life to come.

I knew a young man who was called to the ministry. He was gaining a desirable property. A worldly friend said to him: "You are very foolish to think of giving up all your prospects in life and entering the ministry. Don't you know you will never be worth anything in the world?" "Poor people!" sighed an editor of a secular paper, over Bishop Taylor and his band who are entering Africa. "Poor worldlings," comes back the triumphant retort, "sigh not for us, but for yourselves."

Pharaoh's charge was false. So is every reflection that Satan and his agents would cast upon the truth of God.

Pharaoh's charge was designed to mystify and mislead his bondmen. Precisely so with every insinuation of Satan and his servants against the Gospel of our Lord. He is the great deceiver, and his business is by means fair or foul to hold captive at his will. I heard a convert say shortly since: "I was deceived in regard to religion. Had I known it was so good I would have been a Christian long ago." "Why did you not tell us this before?" has been the exclamation of surprise from many as their deceptions in regard to God's truth have been dispelled. Pharaoh himself was compelled to feel the falsity of his foul accusation. Judgment after judgment fell upon him and his people, and finally more than the terror of all former ones was centered in the final stroke of the "destroying death angel;" and then, convinced of the divine might of the truth and power of the "words" he had derided, "Pharaoh rose up in the night, he and his servants, and all the Egyptians; and there was a great cry in Egypt, for there was not an house where there was not one dead." In the day of final judgment, when all the enemies of Christ and his words shall appear before the great white throne, then in like manner shall their deceptions be triumphantly exposed, and they compelled to bow the knee and confess him King whom they would not as Savior own.

God gave Israel satisfactory proof that his messages to them were divine. The miracles wrought by his servants and the judgment that fell in response to their predictions left no room for doubt in that direction. In like manner the Gospel message is attested by many "infallible signs." The fulfillment of the prophecies of the Old Testament, the teachings, miracles, and resurrection of Jesus, the purity of his life, the fulfillment of his prophecies, the effects of his teaching upon society, the futility of all efforts to crush it, the testimony of thousands of unimpeachable witnesses who have tested its realities in their own experience, and the ever-operating influences of the Holy Spirit, all combine to convince the most skeptical of the divine origin of the message. If one remains unconvinced with all the light of the proof which God has given, it must be because he is either very stupid of head, or persistently perverse of heart.

Pharaoh never helped to bear the burdens that he gave. He said, "Get you unto your burdens," and "Go, therefore, now and work, for there shall no straw be given you, yet shall ye deliver the tale of bricks."

How different from Jesus. He says, "Come unto me, all ye that labor and are heavy laden, and I will give you rest; Take my yoke upon you, and learn of me, for I am meek and lowly in heart, and ye shall find rest to your souls. For my yoke is easy, and my burden is light."

"The load is all gone!" exclaimed a convert as he entered the service of his new Master. Satan, like Pharaoh, increases the burden. Christ lightens or gives strength to joyfully bear it.

The children of Israel were between two contending forces. Pharaoh was determined that they should remain in bondage; and Moses, that they should assert their freedom. So Satan strives mightily for the retention of all beneath his power, while the Savior suffers, dies, intercedes, and sends the Spirit and the Church to struggle for their emancipation. "I feel," said one, "as if I was between two powers, and they were trying to pull me apart."

When Pharaoh saw he could no longer keep Israel, he tried to effect a compromise. He said, "Go ye, sacrifice to your God *in the land.*" Moses replied: "It is not meet so to do." God had commanded that they "go into the wilderness," and Moses had no authority to countermand his order. When Satan sees that his service is about to be forsaken, like Pharaoh, he ever has a plausible appearing compromise to suggest. To one he says, "Be a silent Christian; there is no need of a public profession." To another he says, "No need of prayer; you are strong enough to succeed in your own strength." I have met many who have been duped by the first fallacy, and quite a number by the second. In either instance they remained in bondage.

When one compromise failed, Pharaoh tried another. He said, "I will let you go; only go not very far away." Satan never fails to make a similar trial with all who attempt to leave his service. He, too, says, "I will let you go; only go not very far away." He wants souls to keep within capturing distance. He is quite willing that they should settle down in the village of "Carnal Security;" for his ally, the flesh, knows all the secret approaches to that place, and it will be but a pleasure for him at his leisure to capture them and bring them back. Nor will he make a great ado if they emigrate to the staid little town of "Formality," for he knows that the climate there is so cold that they will soon either freeze to death or return of their own free will. He entreats many, if they must go, to stop in the city of "Worldly Conformity." His ally, the World, has many secret agents here, and he knows full well that all who can be induced to tarry here will not be lost to him.

One morning last Summer I was startled by a sudden knock at the door. I met there a man who said he was sick of sin, and wanted me to come with him at once to the Church and pray for him. I did so, and he seemed to be blessed. He, however, deferred making a more public profession, and soon was back as sadly as ever in bondage. I have known many to "make a start," but, accepting some compromise of Satan, have been loath to leave the ballroom, the racecourse, the circus, cards, and kindred evils, and soon again have been as firmly bound as before in their slavery. To accept any compromise with Satan is invariably to sell out to him.

Failing in the first two, Pharaoh resorts to a third. This is that the men shall go, and leave their families behind. Well aware was he that under such circumstances a pressure which they could not resist would be brought to bear upon them to return. Satan tries the same expedient with those who will forsake his service. He says, "Go if you must; but don't urge your companion, and don't invite your children to go with you, for it will do more hurt than good." Well aware is he that a godless companion and godless children will, if it be possible, draw back to slavery.

The fourth and last compromise was that they should go, but leave their property. Satan always makes a like proposal. He whispers, "It will cost you a great deal to belong to the Church," and is desperate when one sings and acts:

> *Take my silver and my gold,*
> *Not a mite would I withhold.*

When Southern commissioners proposed a compromise in governmental matters to President Lincoln his reply was: "The government must have all." Just so God claims *all* as a condition of spiritual liberation.

Beware of Satan's compromises. They are the web with which he seeks to entangle the escaping soul.

2

In Egypt: Spiritual Bondage (Continued)

Prelude

AND THE BLOOD SHALL be to you for a token upon the houses where ye are, and when I see the blood I will pass over you, and the plague shall not be upon you to destroy you, when I smite the land of Egypt. —Exodus 12:13.

Forasmuch as ye know ye were not redeemed with corruptible things, as silver and gold, from your vain conversation received by tradition from your fathers; but with the precious blood of Christ as of a lamb without blemish and without spot. —1 Peter 1:18-19.

Behold the Lamb of God that taketh away the sin of the world. —John 1:29.

> *Precious, precious blood of Jesus,*
> *Shed on Calvary;*
> *Shed for rebels, shed for sinners,*
> *Shed for me!*
> *Though thy sins are red like crimson,*
> *Deep in scarlet glow,*
> *Jesus' precious blood can make them*
> *White as snow.*

In Egypt: Spiritual Bondage (Continued)

ISRAEL'S DELIVERANCE COULD BE secured only through the offering of blood. A lamb without blemish was to be slain, its blood placed upon the posts of the house. And the Lord said, "The blood shall be to you for a token upon the houses where ye are; and when I see the blood I will pass over you, and the plague shall not be upon you to destroy you when I smite the land of Egypt." The sinner's freedom likewise could be effected only through blood. "Without the shedding of blood there is no remission of sins;" "We have redemption through his blood;" "Forasmuch as ye know, ye were not redeemed with corruptible things, as silver and gold, but with the precious blood of Christ, as of a lamb without blemish and without spot."

> *Common good has common price,*
> *Exceeding good exceeding;*
> *Christ bought the keys of paradise*
> *By cruel bleeding.*

Many have said to me: "I don't see why the shedding of blood should be essential to salvation." A very intelligent man at the close of one of our meetings remained to make some honest inquiries. He had been educated an infidel, but the fact, which he confessed, that Christianity does more for man than infidelity, had led him to stop and candidly investigate its claims and foundations. I said to him in the outset: "If you can have your objections answered and difficulties explained, will you become a Christian at once?" He answered, decidedly: "I will!" God's Spirit wonderfully assisted his servant, and it was only a brief time before he confessed all other difficulties to have vanished, and we were face to face with the question of the "shedding of blood essential to salvation." Our conversation was in substance as follows:

"Do you see the need of a Savior?"

"I do not; it seems to me that if I do right from this time on, that that is all that ought to be required."

"But what about your past sins?"

"I had not thought of them."

"Would it be safe for the State to make the only punishment of law-breakers the promise that they will cease to commit crime, make their wrongs as near right as possible, and henceforth do right?"

"No; the safety of her citizens and the deserts of the criminal both demand that penalties shall be pronounced and executed."

"If that is true of human government, have we not every reason to suppose it is of the divine?"

"We surely have."

"Can you not see, then, that it would not be safe or right for God to remit the penalty because you promise to do better?"

"I never looked at it in this light before, but it does seem so."

"Would it be safe for the State to pardon an offender and restore him to citizenship if he would reform and live right, and in addition to this a substitute could be provided that would have an equal or greater influence in restraining crime as the punishment of the criminal?"

"It seems to me that a pardon might be safely given on such a condition, but on no other."

"Now, do you not see that this is just the sinner's condition?"

"He has broken the laws of the divine government, and in God's sight is a criminal. He has exposed himself to the righteous punishment due to such an offender. For God to indiscriminately pardon such without any substitute for the punishment that would carry equal restraint with its execution, would be to create contempt for his laws, and place a premium on their violation. Imagine a man on trial for some crime. He is proved guilty, but pleads that the sentence shall not be pronounced against him. He gives as his reasons: 1st. That he is sorry that he committed the crime; 2d. That he will do all he can to undo the harm he has done; 3d. That he has not committed many crimes, and has done a great many good deeds; 4th. That he is resolved never to break the law again. What depraved wretch is there that would not profess all of these things if he might clear himself by so doing? But no; the law has been broken, guilt is clearly proved, and the sentence must be served. Justice demands it, and you say, 'Yes, that is right.' Now, if the prisoner is to be saved the penalty of his crime, does he not need a redeemer?"

"It certainly seems so."

"The sinner's case is equally as needy. He has broken divine law. Both himself and his Maker are witness to the fact. He has exposed himself to the sinner's awful penalty, and justice says it must fall. Mercy in the Savior's guise appears, and provides a substitute at infinite cost that will have on thinking beings as strong an influence to deter from sin as the execution of the penalty, and so procures the coming of the Holy Spirit into the soul to assist in living right. The sinner is utterly powerless to procure either the pardon or the Spirit's power; without both he is lost forever. They both are proffered through the blood of Christ, and 'whosoever will' may thus accept them. Do you not see your need of such a Savior?"

"I do."

"Then, will you not here and now accept him?"

"I see no reason why I should not."

After explaining the conditions upon which Christ saves, we kneeled in prayer, and he there and then seemed to fully yield and accept salvation "through the blood."

> *To endless ages let us praise*
> *The precious blood whose price could raise*
> *   The world from wrath and sin;*
> *Whose streams our inward thirst appease,*
> *And heal the sinner's worst disease,*
> *   If he but bathes therein.*
>
> *O, sweetest blood, that can implore*
> *Pardon of God, and heaven restore,*
> *   The heaven which sin had lost;*
> *While Abel's blood for vengeance pleads,*
> *What Jesus shed still intercedes*
> *   For those who wrong him most!*

Salvation through the blood was conditional. They were to sprinkle the "blood upon the door-posts" and "eat the flesh" as God had commanded, or the shed blood would not avail for them. Just so the sinner must meet the conditions upon which pardon is offered through the blood of Christ. Only he that believeth is saved through the blood, and that belief must include complete submission to all of God's requirements. To claim that all will be saved, irrespective of meeting these conditions, were as foolish as to suppose that drowning men for whom a life-boat has been provided will be saved when they stubbornly refuse to enter it.

The children of Israel might have made many excuses for neglecting to accept of deliverance in God's way, but none of them would have been satisfactory. So with the excuses of the sinner. They are the broken ships in which souls are dashed upon the rocks of eternal ruin. They are the bait with which Satan angles for souls. The most specious of them should be shunned as serpents; for though they seek to charm, it is but that they may sting to death eternal. The reader is invited to look and see the absurd folly of the best of them:

1. *"I don't believe in Christ."* All enlightened unbelievers are like the woman at Duplain. She did not believe that the harmless appearing white powder which she swallowed would cause her death; but it did. Unbelief in facts never will alter them.

2. *"I think that all will be saved."* Such resemble the passengers of a sinking ship, who think that all will surely reach the desired port, yet finally perish because they will not get into the lifeboat.

3. *"There are so many hypocrites."* Every one who listens to this plea of Satan is like the man who will not take any pay because there is some counterfeit coin.

4. *"Don't believe in future punishment."* All who sin because of such unbelief are like a man who robs his neighbor because he thinks the government will not execute its laws.

5. *"Am afraid of failing if I start."* To listen to such an excuse would be as foolish as for one who has fallen in the mud to always lie there for fear of again falling.

6. *"I fear I am too wicked."* The one who makes this plea is like the man who won't drink because he is thirsty, or eat because he is hungry, or take medicine because he knows that he is sick. The Savior says that he came to *save* the lost.

7. *"A good moral life is sufficient."* All who reason thus are like children who claim that their duty ends in being kind and honest to each other, without love and obedience to parents.

8. *"It is so hard to break with sinful companions."* How much harder it will be to go on with them to eternal ruin!

9. *"Too much to give up."* All who reject Christ on this account are like the man who, when the ship was sinking, would save his gold at any expense, and so tied it to his waist, and thus by it he was borne to the bottom of the sea. "Too much to give up" cost him his life. It has cost others *life eternal*.

10. *"Waiting for a special call."* That reminds us of a man remaining abed and losing his breakfast because the bell rang for every one instead of each being called by name. *The Gospel "whosoever" rings for all.*

11. *"Cannot understand the Bible."* That is like a child refusing to learn his letters because he cannot read. Christ said, "If any man will do his will he shall know of the doctrine."

12. "*I don't feel like it.*" Silas Badboy did not "feel like it" when it was his duty to ask the teacher's forgiveness and be a good boy, but he had to, or suffer the consequences. So with all who don't feel like submitting to God.

13. "*Too many wrongs to repent of.*" That is like a man who has money enough given him to pay all of his debts, but because there is a great many he won't pay any.

14. "*No time to attend to it.*" All who think so are like a boy who disobeys his parents, and then tries to justify himself by saying he has no time to mind them.

15. "*Cannot make money so fast.*" This excuse is as if a man should hesitate to give up brass for gold and costly diamonds. "What shall it profit a man if he shall gain the whole world and lose his own soul?"

16. "*Tried once and failed.*" Such are like the Mr. Hungry, who, because he tried to get a meal of victuals once and failed, never will try again, but lie down and starve to death.

17. "*So many fail.*" To refuse to yield to Christ on that account would be like resisting the laws of the State, because so many fail to keep them.

18. "*Don't feel deeply enough.*" What is thought of children who disregard the expressed wishes of kind parents, and continually grieve them, and then try to justify themselves by saying, "We would stop it if we only felt deeply enough." If that would be horrible toward earthly parents, how much more so toward our Heavenly Father!

19. "*Religion makes sad and melancholy.*" Yes, just about as much as a pardon does the condemned prisoner, or health the hopeless invalid.

20. "*Was converted once, and believe once in grace, always in grace.*" As well might a clerk who receives certain wages on condition that he earns them, do nothing, and then insist on his pay.

21. "*I am sincere in my unbelief.*" So was the boy who tampered with a loaded rifle; but his sincerity did not save his life.

22. "*I have no concern as to the future.*" Every unconverted person who feels that way is like Mr. Careless who stood unconcerned upon the railroad track when the train was due, and was crushed beneath it.

23. "*I believe God is too good to punish his children hereafter.*" Such forget that we are his children only as we are obedient, otherwise no more so than are devils.

24. "*I belong to the Church.*" But if still unconverted you are like a criminal being borne to prison, who fancies he is safe because he is being carried in a train in which there are good people.

25. "*I am not afraid to die.*" Such unconverted ones are like the man who was not afraid to ride his boat over Niagara Falls. They may go over like him, apparently free from fear, but it is to inevitable ruin, for Christ has declared it.

26. "*Sometime, but not just yet.*" If we make that excuse, we are like a prisoner condemned to death who spurns a pardon purchased for him at great expense; or like a dying man who defers a remedy which, if taken at once, would certainly save his life.

Satan in his efforts to palm off these spurious and damning excuses as real reasons is wonderfully artful and persevering. Take, for instance, the excuse, "I don't feel deeply enough," for an example. He comes and suggests it, and then persistently repeats, it may be a thousand times, "You don't feel deeply enough," etc., until the soul accepts it as the truth, and begins to say, "I don't feel deeply enough," and rests in this lie of the devil as the truth itself. What is true of this excuse is true of everyone with which he ever deceived a human soul. Every cherished excuse that keeps the soul from Christ is the child of Satan and a depraved heart, whose sole business it is to deceive the soul and lead it down into hopeless captivity under the everlasting chains of eternal doom. Spurn as an adder any suggestion that would deter a moment from the renunciation of sin and the acceptance of your Savior and your Lord.

Israel was moved to obey God in part by fear. If they failed to apply the blood, they knew that God would keep his word, and that as certain as the morrow dawned the destroyer would "smite their firstborn," and that they would suffer equally with the Egyptians. We read that in a like manner "Noah, moved with fear, prepared an ark to the saving of his house." So with the sinner. He is led to see his sins and the ruin he has brought upon himself. He looks forward with dread apprehension to death and future judgment. He trembles lest at any moment some sore affliction should be sent for his chastisement. He says to himself: "If I do not soon yield, I feel that God will take my health or children or companion, or blight my business, or perhaps all of these befall me." He remembers that God has said, "Except ye repent ye shall . . . perish;" also, "He that believeth not is condemned already;" and "He that believeth not shall be damned." As these awful facts arise before his face, if he is a rational being, he is afraid.

Some say, "We don't believe in being frightened into religion." They are like a poisoned man who says, "I don't believe in being frightened into taking an antidote." How superlatively nonsensical to be afraid of ordinary calamities, and then tremble not in the presence of infinitely greater spiritual woes! When the sinner, like the prodigal, "comes to himself," he is frightened from sin and ruin to obedience and salvation.

What would be thought of a person in a burning building, who, when he is awakened by the fire bells and alarm of "Fire! Fire!" and exhortations of his friends to escape for his life, should lie still and mutter: "I'm not going to be frightened out of this building." He would be called crazy at once, and yet he would be sane compared with the unconverted person who says, "I am not going to be frightened away from my sins."

Another says, "Don't preach to me of hell and the terrors of the law; I can be won by nothing but love alone." Poor fool! don't you know that the warning you of "hell and the terrors of the law" is one of the kindest deeds of love you ever received? If you have broken God's law and are not concerned in regard to the awful wrong, you are like a man in a burning building, asleep, with the door locked and a powder magazine under him. What greater token of love could such an one receive than for some friend to force the window or the door, and press the alarm until it was heard and acted upon? What would be thought of one thus endangered and warned if he should say, "Let me alone; I don't believe in all this clanging of bells and smashing of windows and excitement on this subject. You need not think that all this, and the crackling of these flames, and your story of the powder magazine, will frighten me up. If you want to win me, you must try and do it by love!" One would almost pity the flames that would be compelled to cremate a wretch so ungrateful. But such an one is sensible compared with him who trifles thus with the messages of the Lord Jesus Christ.

While it is unreasonable for the unpardoned sinner not to fear the awful perils to which he is exposed, and so fear them that he will fly from them, and never sleep until he is assured of safety, yet let it be remembered that afterwards he will learn to serve his new Master, not from fear, but love. While fear is a mighty motive with most in giving up their sins, love should be the mainspring of their after service.

The Israelites partook of the passover prepared for their future journey. They partook of it "with loins girded," "shoes on their feet," "staffs in their hands," and "in haste." This in a marked manner illustrates the way that the sinner should come to Christ. He should come prepared to quickly obey him in everything, for often the "King's business requires haste," and he should be ready to "run the way of his commandment." His life henceforth is to be a pilgrimage, and his "loins" should be "girt about with truth," and "feet shod with the preparation of the Gospel of peace." He should "lay aside every weight," that he may able to "run with patience the race set before him."

God's people were accompanied from Egypt by a "mixed multitude." Moved by various motives, many of the Egyptians went with them. In a like manner people sometimes unite with the visible Church who are spiritual Egyptians at heart. I knew a party who made pretensions to piety until he had secured an alliance with a religious lady, when he professed no more. Others may have made like pretensions to "help their business." Members of a Church in a certain place are in the habit of saying to persons coming to their town, whose membership they desire: "If you want to move in the best society you will have to join our Church." Some under such a pressure, doubtless, have been induced to unite, to gain social position.

"A great many who started in the last revival have gone back again," is a statement heard sometimes in regard to revival work. The fact is sometimes mentioned as if the fault was with the revivalist or the pastor or the Church. The blame may sometimes rest with them, but the "mixed multitude" idea will more frequently explain it. No one should be surprised at the falling away of many after a great Gospel ingathering. It always has been, and always will be so.

The Savior anticipated and explained this in his parable of the "sower and the seed." There were then, are now, and ever will be where the Gospel seed is sown, "good ground," "thorny ground," and "wayside hearers." This fact should not discourage the Gospel worker, but stimulate him to do all that lies within his power to redeem from the wayside, remove the "stones" and destroy the "thorns," so that any failure may not be because of his neglect. While much seed and labor may seem to be lost, yet God stimulates every worker with the glad assurance, "So shall my word be that proceedeth out of my mouth; it shall not return unto me void, but it shall accomplish that which I please, and it shall prosper in the thing whereto I send it."

God guided the Israelites from the beginning of their journey. "And the Lord went before by day in the pillar of a cloud, and by night in a pillar of fire, to give them light to go by day and night." Just so from the minute that the sinner turns from sin God will guide him. He will make the way so plain before his obedient feet that he need not miss it. The Spirit and the Word, by day and by night, will guide from the Egypt of sin to the highlands of holiness.

They went out in haste. So with the sinner. For a long time he may be "thinking about" his condition; but the time comes, when, startled by the surgings of death's overflow stream, or the black storm cloud of past transgressions, or the flash of the sword of justice, or the frown of an offended God, or the lashes of a guilty conscience, or the gleam of the great white judgment throne, or the tragical picture of awaiting doom, or the fiery furnace of affliction, or the dawning of the great eternity, or all of these things combined, he, like Bunyan's Christian, turns his back to the City of Destruction, and "flies from the wrath to come, and lays hold on eternal life."

In attempting to escape from Egypt they were pursued by Pharaoh and his followers. When the Israelites saw themselves at the mercy of Pharaoh and his men of might, we read that "they were sore afraid." They doubtless thought that, now they had left Egypt, Pharaoh would molest them no more. Vain delusion! With intensified wrath he pursues, and now threatens their utter annihilation. Their condition seems worse than when slaves in Egypt. The seeking sinner often feels as they did. "I feel a good deal worse than when the revival began," said one under this impulse.

While they were quiet in Egypt, Pharaoh knew they were in his power; but now he sees that he is losing his victims, and hence his fierce onset for their recovery. So with Satan. While we are quietly living in the world, and making no especial effort to escape, Satan is comparatively quiet, but when once the world is renounced and we claim the freedom proffered by the Savior, then the devil pursues with all his hounds. Mr. Moody relates the following, which forcibly illustrates the thought under consideration: "Sam," said an infidel judge, "how is it that you Christians are always talking about the conflicts you have with Satan? I am better off than you are. I don't have any conflicts or trouble, and yet I am an infidel, and you are a Christian — always in a muss. How's that, Sam?"

This floored the colored man for awhile. He did not know how to meet the old infidel's argument. So he shook his head sorrowfully and said, "I dunno, massa, I dunno."

The judge always carried a gun along with him for hunting. Pretty soon they came to a lot of ducks. The judge took his gun and blazed away at them, and wounded one and killed another. The judge said quickly, "You jump in, Sam, and get that wounded duck before he gets off," and did not pay any attention to the dead one. In went Sam for the wounded duck, and came out reflecting.

The colored man then thought he had an illustration. He said to the judge: "I hab him now, massa; I'se able to show you how de Christian hab de greater conflict dan de infidel. Don't you know de moment you wounded dat ar duck how anxious you was to get 'im out, and you did not care for de dead duck, but just left 'im alone?"

"Yes," said the judge.

"Well," said Sam, "you see how dat ar dead duck's a sure thing. I'se wounded, and I tries to get away from de debbil. It takes trouble to kotch me, but, massa, you're a dead duck; dar is no squabble for you. The debbil have you sure!"

Pharaoh was foiled because the people "cried to God" for help. In a like manner the escaping sinner may ever triumph over his spiritual foes. "Resist the devil, and he will flee from you." He is a coward, and will run if resisted. May each forsake his service forever!

3

The Red Sea: Spiritual Deliverance

Prelude

HE REBUKED THE RED Sea also, and it was dried up: so he led them through the depths, as through the wilderness. And he saved them from the hand of him that hated them, and redeemed them from the hand of the enemy. And the waters covered their enemies: there was not one of them left. Then believed they his words; they sang his praise. —Psalms 106:9-12.

If therefore the Son shall make you free, ye shall be free indeed. —John 8:36.

> *The chains that have bound me are flung to the wind;*
> *By the mercy of God the poor slave is set free;*
> *And the strong grace of heaven breathes strong o'er the mind,*
> *Like the bright waves of Summer that gladden the sea.*

The Red Sea: Spiritual Deliverance

MANY OF THE EVENTS occurring at this point in the history of this people are vividly illustrative of those which occur with the sinner at the point of conversion.

The darkness of despair was immediately followed by the light of deliverance. Sweeping down upon them from behind and like a terrific whirlwind, was one of the world's mightiest armies, exasperated and thirsting for blood, and led by victors of many a battlefield, headed by one of earth's mightiest kings, himself furious with rage. Before them, and now at their very feet, like a bottomless abyss, the Red Sea seems waiting to swallow them up. Their condition seems to be without one ray of hope. To go back is sure ruin, to stand still is to be crushed by Pharaoh's power, and to go ahead is to meet with what seems to be an insurmountable difficulty.

Just so with the sinner when he comes to the point of full surrender. To go back or to stand still is to fall a wretched victim to Satan's cruel and deceptive rage; while to obey God and go forward is to meet with what seems to be some difficulty that cannot be conquered. When I reached that point the agony was intense. I dare not go back, I dare not stand still; but when I looked forward there lay right in the direction of my longed for liberty a duty that it seemed to me I could never do. I was about to teach school and the Spirit said, "You ought to read and pray before your pupils." Satan said, "You can't do that," and he repeated this so often and with such vehemence that I for a time believed him. It was my Red Sea.

Sometimes, as in my case, it is some one thing, and with others it is many things. Sometimes it is a confession of wrong words said, or wrong deeds done, or forgiving the wrongs of others, or restitutions to make, or kindred things; and with others the struggle comes in a more general way over the question of total surrender in all things to God. In either case Satan attempts to make the molehill look like a mountain, and the drop like a shoreless ocean; and whether he marshals his forces and attacks every part of the being at once, or concentrates them with focalized fury at the weakest point, as he did with me, it matters not, for in either case he will do all that lies within his power to make advancement seem impossible.

Just now a lady called, feeling that she "must have help or die." The darkness of despair was settling over her, but she went "forward," and her Red Sea opened, light broke in, and freedom sweet was found. Just at the point of Israel's utter despair there came the joyful message: "Fear ye not; stand still and see the salvation of the Lord which he will show you today, for the Egyptians ye have seen today, ye shall see them again no more forever. The Lord shall fight for you, and ye shall hold your peace." Then came the command, "Go forward!" and quickly they were free, and all their enemies destroyed. The black, black night of bitter bondage suddenly gave place to the bright, bright day of long-hoped-for liberty.

Thus suddenly may the sinner be translated from the power of darkness into the marvelous light of spiritual day. Saul of Tarsus was, and millions likewise. You may; it is God's will and your privilege.

The people reached a place where they could do nothing but "stand still and see the salvation of the Lord." Precisely so with the seeker of Christ. He reaches a place where he confesses and forsakes all sin, and fully surrenders to God; where he sees that nothing but the power of God can save him; where he sings:

> *Nothing in my hands I bring;*
> > *Simply to the cross I cling;*

where he sees that none but Jesus has power to pardon a single sin; where he remembers that God says, "Let the wicked forsake his way, and the unrighteous man his thought, and let him return unto the Lord, and he will have mercy on him, and unto our God for he will abundantly pardon," and feels that he has forsaken all wicked ways and renounced all evil thoughts, and returned as a suppliant suing for mercy to his kingly Father, and has now nothing more that he can do but expectantly "look" for the bestowment of the pardon promised. He says, "I'll keep surrendered and keep looking until salvation I shall see." He feels:

> *Weeping will not save me;*
> > *Though my face were bathed in tears;*
> > *That could not allay my fears,*
> > *Could not wash the sins of years—*
> *Weeping will not save me.*

> *Working will not save me;*
> > *Purest deeds that I can do,*
> > *Holiest thoughts and feelings, too,*
> > *Cannot form my soul anew*
> *Working will not save me.*

So he turns from all else to Christ, and, obediently "looking" to him, he becomes conscious of his great salvation.

"*By faith* they passed through the Red Sea as by dry land, which the Egyptians assaying to do, were drowned." (Heb. 9:29.) There are several particulars in which the faith of the people at this place is like the faith that must be exercised at conversion.

It was an obedient faith. Its exercise was preceded and attended by complete surrender to God's will. They had left Egypt at his word, and were ready to undertake to do the seemingly impossible, should he command it. Likewise, the seeker for pardon must, in order to exercise the faith that brings it, confess and forsake all sin, and pledge allegiance to his Savior King. Some have simply "turned over a new leaf," "reformed in some particulars," "went forward," "been baptized," "asked for prayers," or, perhaps, united with some Church; and then, because they had done these things, wondered why it was that they could not exercise the faith that would bring the knowledge of sins forgiven.

Such acts are good and helpful if rightly used, but can never be substituted instead of the clearly revealed conditions on which, and only on which, the King and government of heaven the pardon offers; *i. e.*, full confession and renunciation of sin, and sworn allegiance to God and his government. When this condition is met, then the exercise of faith in God's promises of salvation is just as easy as breathing.

I tried for weeks to believe myself into salvation when I was trying to dodge the question of praying in my school, but I miserably failed; but when I fully yielded at that last point I could not help believing, and the sweet peace of a soul forgiven was mine. God save us from trying to "dodge" issues insisted on by our Maker! He who is trying to believe that God pardons him when he is not meeting the terms upon which salvation is offered to all, is guilty of presumption, which, if persisted in, will bring certain ruin.

It was a rational faith. It rested not in conjecture or feeling, but in a definite promise given by God himself. God had said to Moses:

"Lift up thy rod, and stretch out thine hand over the sea ... and the children of Israel shall go over on dry ground." They believed that the conditions being met, God would do just what he had agreed to, and acted accordingly. God in many places expressly promises to pardon all who will forsake sin and obey him.

It is as if a father of unquestionable integrity should write to his wayward son saying: "If you will reform and come home, I will pardon you, and treat you as my son again." The boy has a definite promise, and it would be unreasonable for him to disbelieve it; and trusting that, he comes expecting to receive the proffered pardon. It having been made possible by the sacrifice of Christ for God to do so, he solemnly promises to grant a full pardon to all who meet the plainly stated terms upon which it is offered.

To disbelieve that he is true to his offer, when we meet the conditions, is to offer him an infinite insult. If it is unreasonable to doubt the veracity of a man of established integrity, how much more so to doubt the truthfulness of Him who is the truth, and whose every promise is as changeless as himself!

I have read somewhere of a man who was led into the light by his employer. At first the way of faith seemed dark to him, and, hoping to help him, his master sent him a note, asking him to come and see him at six o'clock. He came promptly, with the letter in his hand. When ushered into his room, his master inquired, "Do you wish to see me, James?"

James was confounded, and holding up the note requesting him to come, said, "The letter! the letter!"

"O," said the master, "I see you believe I wanted to see you, and when I sent you the message you came at once?"

"Surely, sir! Surely, sir!" replied James.

"Well, see! here is another letter, sent by one equally as earnest," said his master, holding up a slip of paper with some texts of Scripture written upon it.

James took the paper, and began to read slowly: "Come unto me all ye that labor," etc. His lips quivered, his eyes filled with tears, and, like to choke with emotion, he thrust his hand into his jacket pocket, grasping his large red handkerchief, with which he covered his face, and there he stood for a few moments, not knowing what to do. At length he inquired, "Am I just to believe that in the same way that I believed your letter?"

"Just in the same way," rejoined his master. This expedient was owned of God in setting James at liberty. He was a happy believer that very night, and has continued to go on his way rejoicing in God his Savior, to point others to Cavalry and walk in the narrow way.

It was an expectant faith. At God's command they marched right forward with safety in the midst of the sea, and God's power thus was to be made manifest. Just so we must come for pardon, expecting it just as much as the hungry child expects his food at mealtime, and verily we shall not be disappointed. Red Seas will divide, mountains will crumble, and we, by faith, shall overcome. Hallelujah!

It was a personal faith. They made sure that they met the conditions, and that the promise was to them, and then expected themselves to realize the great salvation. If John simply believes that the promises are for all in general, and not for himself in particular, he will not get the blessing. He must believe that they are for himself as much as if he were the only one on earth. The devil is after him, sin is ruining him, hell is greedy for him, friends are praying for him, the Spirit is striving with him, Jesus died for him, and every promise of salvation in the Bible is for him; and he must make a personal matter of it, or all avails him naught.

It was a present faith. They believed that, there and then, God would undertake for them as he had agreed. Satan is satisfied if he can induce one to say, "I believe God will save some time," and rest there. I am to believe on the authority of God's changeless Word that, just now while I am meeting the conditions upon which he sees fit to offer to save me, he is saving.

Of all who exercise such a faith as that above described it is written: "He that believeth on the Son *hath* everlasting life;" "According to their faith, so it is unto them;" "Watch vigilantly, lest Satan deceive you with a spurious faith." May we each exercise an obedient, rational, expectant, personal, and present faith in the blood that buys our forgiveness and frees from Satan's thralldom!

Their deliverance was all of God. He called them, led them, defeated and destroyed their foes, and made the path through the sea for their salvation. So with the sinner. God awakens, stimulates, strives, pleads, bleeds, and saves, and man simply yields and follows.

With Israel at this point it was a question of escaping danger more than of future service. They feared Pharaoh and his hosts, and this was a mighty motive which moved them the action. With many the beginning of the Christian life is similar to this. They fear that they

> *Can but perish if they go,*
> *And are resolved to try,*
> *For if they stay away they know*
> *They shall forever die.*

As Noah, moved with fear, prepared an ark to the saving of his house, so many, moved by fear of an impending and eternal doom, prepare to meet their God, and seek that love through which duty becomes delight.

The Red Sea commemorated a great deliverance. The power of Pharaoh and Egypt was broken, and Israel, delivered from these enemies, was God's people. When the sinner is converted he meets with a like change. His past sins are all forgiven, the power of Satan and the world is broken, and he becomes a child of God. The change is so marvelous that no language can express it.

Israel had satisfactory evidence that this deliverance was real.

First: They had God's Word for it.

Second: They saw the defeat of their enemies.

Third: They saw with their own eyes that they were not in Egypt.

First: The converted man has similar evidence. As soon as he meets the conditions of salvation he has God's Word for it that he is saved. "Do you believe you are saved?" said a saint to a seeker. "I have not the evidence I want," said he; "I have nothing but the Word for it." "Nothing but the Word!" What a blasphemous impeachment of the veracity of the Most High! Rather let the obedient, trusting soul say, "I have the Word of my Maker that he is saving me, and in that will I trust forever. The earth shall melt, the heavens vanish, and all things seen shall disappear, but the Word of my God shall endure forever. In that I trust, and trusting, feel as secure as a sunbeam resting in the mighty ocean." Then can he sing—

> *In his Word I am trusting, assurance divine!*
> *I'm hoping no longer· I know he is mine.*

He that thus believeth will have "the witness in himself."

Second: They will see the defeat of their enemies. When Satan tempts he will be resisted, and old habits will be conquered, and all enemies overcome.

Third: "Old things will have passed away, and all things become new." New hopes, new joys, new friends, new books, new papers, new homes, new habits, all will attest the wondrous change from darkness unto light, and the soul sees the difference just as clearly as Israel saw the crystal walls of water that rose on either side.

At this point they were "baptized unto Moses," and here the newly saved, having forsaken the "world, the flesh, and the devil," are "baptized unto Jesus."

As they each hereafter were identified with God's visible Church, so will each one delivered from spiritual Egypt unite with some branch of his Church below, and by God's grace be an earnest worker in the same.

Red Sea of spiritual deliverance! Thou art the birthplace of our souls into a kingdom all of whose glories even eternity will be unable to unfold, and as such we will commemorate thee forever.

Dear reader, if you have not already done so, I plead with you to settle this matter *just now. This moment* renounce the Egypt of sin, and, accepting soul liberty through our Savior, place your name upon the "Roll of Liberty and Life," and by God's grace sign before you lay down the book, and ever keep the accompanying pledge.

If you will do this, you will please God, be true to yourself, save your own soul, and doubtless win many others. Then, also, you will be prepared to gladly accompany us as we hasten on to Canaan's summits, that, rising in the distance, even now invite our tarrying feet.

If you put it off, you will wrong your Maker, your fellow man, and yourself; will do violence to your reason, harden your conscience, insult your Savior, grieve and, perhaps, forever quench the Holy Spirit, dare future judgment, invite affliction, and, perhaps, bring upon yourself a death and eternity as tragical as the following:

> A young man, at the close of a religious service, was asked to decide the matter of his soul's salvation. He said, "I will not do it tonight."
>
> Well, the Christian man kept talking with him, and he said, "I insist that tonight you either take God or reject him."
>
> "Well," said the young man, "if you put it that way I will reject him. There now, the matter's settled." On his way home on horseback, he knew not that a tree had fallen aslant the road, and he was going at full speed, and he struck the obstacle and dropped lifeless.
>
> That night his Christian mother heard the riderless horse plunging about the barn, and suspecting that something terrible was the matter, she went out and came to the place where her son lay, and she cried out, *"O, Henry! dead, and not a Christian! O, my son! my son! dead, and not a Christian! O, Henry! Henry! dead, and not a Christian!"*

Or should your life be spared, and salvation later still be offered, it may be with you as it was with one in a terrible storm on Lake Michigan. Hope of safety had faded from every heart, and each moment a watery grave was expected. One who was there endangered was afterwards asked if he did not then feel like praying? "No," he said, "*I could not believe that God would hear me.*"

Or you may finally feel as the old man did when urged to make the long-deferred choice. He answered, "No, I cannot do it now; *it would be offering the dregs of my life to God.*"

After attending one of our meetings a man dreamed that he saw an angel in his room, holding in its hand a weight suspended by a cord, a strand of which was broken. Then it seemed to him as if the angel said, "*This is the brittle thread of thy life.*" O, unsaved one! This passing opportunity may be the brittle thread upon which hangs thy life eternal. Don't neglect it!

May you now decide, as you will wish you had when the death damp is gathering on your brow, and when, to give an account for this moment's decision, you stand before the great white throne!

ROLL OF LIBERTY AND LIFE

If the Son, therefore, shall make you FREE, ye shall be free indeed. John 8:36.

CHRIST

I am ... the Life. —John 11:25.

ANGELS

When the Son of man shall come in his glory and all his holy ANGELS, then shall he sit on the throne of his glory. —Matt. 26:46.

THE RIGHTEOUS

But the RIGHTEOUS into life eternal.

—Matt. 25:46.

THE SAVED

The nations of them which are SAVED shall walk in the light of it. —Rev. 21:24.

THE OBEDIENT

He became the author of eternal salvation unto all them that OBEY him. —Heb. 5:9.

BELIEVERS

He that BELIEVETH and is baptized shall be saved. —Mark 16:16.

THE PENITENT

There is joy in the presence of the angels of God over one sinner that REPENTETH. —Luke 15:1.

THE CONVERTED

The law of the Lord is perfect, converting the soul. —Psa. 19:5.

THE TRIUMPHANT

Rejoice because your names are written in heaven. —Luke 10:20.

Name _____

Eternal Life

ROLL OF BONDAGE AND DEATH

Whosoever committeth sin is the SERVANT of sin. —John 8:34.

SATAN

And the DEVIL that deceived them was cast into the lake of fire. —Rev. 20:10.

DEVILS

Prepared for the devil and his ANGELS. —Matt. 25:41.

HYPOCRITES

And appoint him his portion with HYPO-CRITES. There shall be weeping and gnashing of teeth. —Matt. 25:51.

THE UNSAVED

And THESE shall go away into EVERLASTING punishment. —Matt.25:46.

THE DISOBEDIENT

For which thing's sake cometh the wrath of God upon the children of DISOBEDIENCE. —Col. 3:6.

UNBELIEVERS

He that BELIEVETH not shall he damned. —Mark 16:16.

He that BELIEVETH not is condemned already.

THE IMPENITENT

Except ye REPENT ye shall all likewise perish. —Luke 13:3.

THE UNCONVERTED

Except ye be CONVERTED ... ye shall not enter into the kingdom of heaven.

—Matt. 18:3.

THE LOST

And whosoever was not found written in the Book of Life was cast into the lake of fire. —Rev. 20:15.

Name _____

Eternal Death

ON WHICH ROLL IS YOUR NAME?

LIBERTY AND LIFE PLEDGE

I do repent of all my sins, accept of Christ on *His terms,* and purpose henceforth, with His help, to serve Him and ever keep my name on the "Roll of Liberty and Life."

Name _____

Residence _____

Date _____

"O that beautiful city, with its mansions of light;

With its glorified beings in pure garments of white,

Where no evil thing cometh to despoil what is fair,

Where the angels are watching—*yes, my name's written there!*"

4

The Sinai Wilderness: Spiritual Twilight

Prelude

MOREOVER THOU LEDDEST them in the day by a cloudy pillar; and in the night by a pillar of fire, to give them light in the way wherein they should go. Thou camest down also upon Mount Sinai, and spakest with them from heaven, and gavest them right judgments and true laws, good statutes and commandments. And gavest them bread from heaven for their hunger, and broughtest forth water for them out of the rock for their thirst, and promised at them that they should go in to possess the land which thou hadst sworn to give them. —Neh. 9:12, 13, 15.

For as many as are led by the Spirit of God, they are the sons of God. —Romans 8:14.

And I, brethren, could not speak unto you as unto spiritual, but as unto carnal, even as unto babes in Christ. —Col. 3:1.

> Are you shining for Jesus, dear one?
> You have given your heart to him;
> But is the light strong within it,
> Or is it but pale and dim?
> Can everybody see it
> That Jesus is all to you?
> That your love to him is burning
> With radiance warm and true?
> Is the seal upon your forehead,
> So that it must be known
> That you are all for Jesus,
> That your heart is all his own?

The Sinai Wilderness: Spiritual Twilight

PLACE: ROUTE OF ISRAEL from the Red Sea to Kadesh Barnea, on the border of Canaan. Many of the events occurring here vividly illustrate those which occur in the lives of believers between the time when they

are converted and that when they come to the point of receiving or re-
jecting the fullness of the Holy Ghost. This may be called the Sinai Wilderness experience, and should not be confounded with the Desert Wilderness experience, which began after the defeat at Kadesh. *That* is a
photograph of the life of the backslider, *this* of the converted believer.

The devil displays great cunning in his efforts to persuade many of his
victims that they are in this, when in truth they are in that. Beware of his
devices!

*In this section of their journey they sang songs of conscious deliver-
ance, exclaiming:* "The Lord is my strength and my song, and is become
my salvation." In the parallel experience at times the converted soul "cannot keep from singing,"

> *Hallelujah! 'tis done, I believe on the Son;*
> *I am saved by the blood of the Crucified One,*

or kindred songs of the soul's redemption. Often there will be "songs in
the night," and "music in the soul."

*Israel here had broken loose from the control, service, and dominions
of Pharaoh.* In a like manner all justified believers have forsaken the
service, control, and dominions of Satan. Knowing that "whoso
committeth sin is the servant of sin," and that he that committeth sin is of
the devil, and that "of whom a man is overcome, of the same is he brought
in bondage," and that "no man can serve two masters, for either he will
hate the one and love the other, or else he will hold to the one and despise
the other," they have "renounced the devil and all his works," and will,
knowingly, do nothing that will please him. If surprised into such an act,
they are deeply pained, and at once sincerely repent and claim forgiveness. They also "renounce" the "vain pomp and glory of this world,"
with all covetous desires of the same, so that they will not follow or be
led by them.

What a sadly ridiculous spectacle for those who have done this to be
at the theater, Sunday excursion, racecourse, circus, rink, card table, raffle,
or kindred places; thus acting a huge lie, and proving by their support of
these soul-traps of the devil that they are either hypocrites or deluded!
Such are as far from the Sinai Wilderness experience as darkness is from

light. Whenever Satan is unable to secure the rejection of the Gospel, his next effort is to lower its standard. He, therefore, attempts to substitute "a good moral life," or a "nominal Church membership," for justification, justification for entire sanctification, and make his dupes believe that this can be gained only after the deathline. He has succeeded so well that many professors are appalled at the Bible picture of a justified life, and find themselves in spiritual Egypt instead of the Sinai Wilderness experience of justifying grace. Had they considered this subject with a fraction of the force expended by them upon worldly themes, long since would they have seen the fallacies in which their surface thinking has ensnared them.

They were God's people just as truly as when in Canaan. In a like manner are all who have really crossed the Red Sea of conversion and are pressing Canaanward. They have a title to heaven, and unless they forfeit it, are sure to get there. Before their conversion they were spiritually dead; now they are alive, and when they enter Canaan they will be strong.

During this part of their journey they received especial preparatory instruction. By miracles and judgments, by the manna for food, and the cloud and pillar of fire for guidance, by the giving of the law and the construction of the tabernacle at Mt. Sinai, by the vestments of the priests, the ceremonies and furniture of the tabernacle, and the clear teachings of Moses and his assistants, they were instructed as to their own need, the nature of God, and the blessedness of doing the divine will. Likewise all who are converted are taught of God. They learn of Jesus. They are "disciples," and grow rapidly in the knowledge of themselves and God's claims upon them, their privileges, and wonderful possibilities under grace. The spiritual Sinai Wilderness is the "preparatory department" to the Canaan "university course."

They were fed with bread from heaven. Likewise God feeds the least of them that love him with the "bread that cometh from above." He who does not love to meditate upon the Word of God may know by this that he is not a pardoned man.

They were placed under a teacher who, in a good sense of that phrase, "made holiness a hobby." Moses preached it in every sermon; he preached it whether "men would hear or forbear;" he preached it "strongly, constantly, and explicitly." How like Jesus, the teacher of the justified, who repeatedly asserts that only those who "do the will" "shall enter the kingdom," and prays, "Sanctify them through thy truth," and positively prohibits his apostles from their lifework until within them the "promise of the Father" is fulfilled, and they receive "power from on high."

The blood of "sprinkling," the awful "curses" attached to the violation of the law, the " blessings" connected with its keeping, and the many exhortations received to "sanctify themselves," and " be holy," all continually reminded them of their obligation to live a holy life.

So with all who have forsaken the service of Satan. A holy God in the form of the Holy Father, Holy Son, and Holy Spirit, through the Holy Word and a holy ministry, keep constantly before them the deep need of holiness of heart and life. They feel its need, long for its attainment, and seek to enter into its blessedness. Though not yet in the Canaan of perfect love, they "earnestly desire" there to be. They frequently feel as one did who witnessed: "One day, while in this state, I went into a holiness meeting, and the songs and the faces of the people who sang them, struck conviction through me. I came up to Kadesh Barnea, looked over into the promised land, and wanted to get in." "Hatred" of Bible holiness is never found in those who are truly justified, but among backsliders, professors who never were converted, and other dwellers in the swamps of spiritual Egypt.

God called his people "out of Egypt" that he might lead them "into Canaan." Likewise we are called "out of darkness" "into light," out of "uncleanness" into "holiness," and have been "chosen in him before the foundation of the world, that we should be holy and without blame before him."

They were earnest workers. They built the tabernacle and discharged the other duties connected with the life they were living. Likewise all who are living in the light of justifying grace will be found as "workers with God." To cease to work for God is to forfeit pardon. Laziness is as wicked in God's sight as profanity. "Do nothing" people must get out of Egypt before they can get into Canaan.

They made foolish prayers. God answered, and "gave them the desire of their heart, but sent leanness to their souls." It was when the disciples were in this stage of their experience that they wanted to call for fire from heaven to consume their enemies, and asked for the "first place" in the Savior's kingdom.

A brother minister's little boy was overheard to pray: "O God, do send me a little brother." In about a month the little brother came, but was very weak and cross. The little fellow was greatly disappointed, and after restraining his pent-up feelings for some time, exclaimed, "O dear, I would not have asked God for a little brother if I had known he would have been so cross!"

Many have insisted upon riches, to the ruination of their souls. Others, like the little boy who prayed, "Lord, let me live to be ninety years old, and as much more as you think best," have prayed for long life, and then, like him, have lived to lament their folly. Others have insisted that God should spare the lives of their children, and then, like the mother who did so and afterward saw the selfsame son die a murderer upon the gallows, have learned too late that God's way was best. We know not what we should pray for as we ought, and it is only when we live in constant communion with that Spirit who "maketh intercession according to the will of God," that we will be able at all times to pray wisely.

In spiritual Egypt there is no real prayer. In the Sinai Wilderness experience there are many unwise prayers. In spiritual Canaan there is the fervent and effectual prayer that "availeth much."

They were "out of Egypt" but not "into Canaan." Likewise God's people may be out of the Egypt of sin, but not into the Canaan of the Spirit's power. Such was the condition of Isaiah before his lips were touched with the "live coal;" the Disciples prior to Pentecost; Fletcher, Wesley, Mrs. Edwards, Earl, Upham, Bishop Hamline, Harrison, Moody, and a host of others, for a period after crossing the Red Sea of conversion.

They were unduly influenced by the mixed multitude. In a similar way, without the Spirit's fullness, the believer will be unduly swayed by the wishes and opinions of the surrounding unsaved. Pandering to such influences, God's people have sometimes permitted that to be practiced in his name and for his service that has brought odium instead of blessing. The demand for ungodly choristers and choirs, for preaching that will please and never offend, for restraint to be thrown over audible responses in religious meetings, for questionable expedients for raising money for religious purposes, for trashy literature in the Sunday-school and the home, and kindred encroachments on the purity of the Gospel, comes in a great degree from this source.

They were inclined to live on old manna. To their disgust it soon "bred worms." The same is true of believers in the parallel experience. They sometimes foolishly attempt to work today on the strength of yesterday, or fondly look backward to a past experience instead of upward for a present one. They fail to constantly claim fresh manna from above.

They were honored and encouraged by frequent expressions of divine favor. The daily manna, the quenching of their thirst, victory over their enemies, the pillar of cloud and of fire, and many other heavenly tokens told them that they were God's and that he was kindly caring for them.

So with all who are truly justified. Frequent feasts of "food" from above, and drafts from the river of the "water" of life, increasing victories over the enemies of the soul, and occasional manifestations of the divine presence, all show clearly that the new life is imparted in the soul; and, like the apostles before their entrance into the Canaan of perfect love, they have been with Jesus on the mountain of transfiguration, often have sat at his feet as humble pupils, and know that, though Canaan still lies before them, yet still their "names are written in heaven."

They were thoroughly organized. They "came out" from Egypt, but they did not "come out" from each other. Although there were bad persons among both the people and the priests, yet this did not prevail as an excuse for "coming out." This analogy should, doubtless, ever hold good where the religious organization, like the Church at that time, is subject to divine direction.

The "come-out-ism" that prevails in some sections reminds of "John and his wife," who had, with quite a body, seceded from a Church, and then, with others, separated from the seceding body, and continued the process until they were the only ones left. It is said that then she was asked concerning the true Church, and her reply was, "I believe that we have the true religion and are the true Church, only I sometimes have my doubts about John."

In this stage of their history their spiritual vision was dim. Like the blind man before his complete healing, they could see, but not clearly. Hence they said and did a great many foolish and short-sighted things that clear vision would have prevented, and in regard to which second thought brought sorrow. The like is emphatically true of most, between the time of their conversion and when they enter into the experience of entire sanctification. Though followers and learners of Jesus, their eyes are "holden" that they do not see clearly the deep spiritual things of the kingdom. Spiritual cleansing, and power, and holiness seem desirable to them, but are sought indefinitely, and seem to be seen as through a mist. Egypt is "darkness," Sinai Wilderness is "dim sight," Canaan is "perfect vision."

They kept the ordinances of the Church. The Sabbath day, the holy convocations, and all other divine regulations were sacredly regarded. In a similar way will the true believer regard Christian duties and privileges. Scripture-searching, family and private prayer, prayer, experience, Sunday school, sacramental, and preaching services will be regularly regarded. Duty will not be delighted in as when the Canaan experience has been reached, *but it will be done just as certainly as then.*

Wrong was abandoned as soon as detected. Their dim vision and weaknesses caused them many times to fall; but instead of keeping down or wandering off to remain in forbidden ways, they arose and pressed onward. So with all who remain truly justified. Though they sometimes fall, yet they seek at once God's pardoning favor, arise, and triumphantly exclaim: "Rejoice not against me, O mine enemy; when I fall I shall arise!" The time is near when they will learn the secret of "standing," and "having done all to stand;" but until then, though they "fall seven times a day," yet will they arise again. If, like Peter, they deny their Lord one moment, like him they repent with bitter tears the next.

In this part of their journey they laid aside the ornaments which they wore in Egypt. "And the children of Israel stripped themselves of their ornaments by Mount Horeb." (Ex. 33:6.) In a similar way many believers, in this "twilight" of their religious life, have seen adorning with "gold, pearls, and costly array" (1 Tim. 2:9; 1 Peter 3:3), to be contrary to good taste and the teachings and spirit of the Gospel, and have laid them all aside. The Israelites put their adornments into the "church building fund." Their brethren and sisters today often put theirs there, or in the "missionary box," and in either case God is pleased.

They leaned too much on human helps. In the absence of Moses on the mount they fell. There is a like tendency on the part of most Christians who are not in Canaan. Dissensions in the Church, changes in the order of worship, the fall of the professedly pious, the removal of their favorite pastor, cross words where kind have been looked for, and kindred causes, unduly move them, because their trust is too much in things below. "I go fishing," and "We go, too," was the cry of Peter and his company in this stage of their experience, when hopes which they had been cherishing seemed shaken. They have had their kindred in all centuries.

They gave liberally for God's work. They responded so freely for the construction of the tabernacle that it was said, "The people bring much more than enough for the service of the work which the Lord commanded to make;" and it was needful to restrain their offerings. A justified state that does not bear kindred fruit should be viewed with suspicion. Unconverted people may be liberal, and sometimes are; really justified ones surely will be, although their motives in being so are often mixed; fully sanctified ones always will be, and *gladly*, and with *pure motives*. To be a "stingy professor " is possible, but to be a "stingy possessor" of divine love would be as impossible as to be an honest thief. Stingy professors must get out of Egypt before they can get into Canaan.

Wherein they wronged anyone they were bound to make confession and restitution, if in their power. The hope of a professedly justified man that will not do likewise is a fatal delusion.

As they were cut loose from Egypt, so is the real Christian cut loose from the world. He no longer loves the world. He has renounced it. Well aware is he that "if any man love the world, the love of the Father is not in him." "Brother―― is a splendid Christian, with the exception that he is very worldly," said a leader of a prominent member in his Church. With just as much truth and sense might it have been said in the day of civil war, "Mr.―― is a splendidly loyal man, with the exception that he is a rank rebel." In spiritual Egypt the World is "served" and "loved;" in a justified life it is "renounced;" and in an entirely sanctified life it is "hated" and "triumphantly overcome."

In this part of the journey Israel was in spiritual babyhood. The nation was born but very babyish. So with converted people who stop short of full salvation. They may be mental, moral, social, and ecclesiastical giants, but *spiritually* they will be babes. They must needs be fed milk instead of meat, and often prefer being rocked in the cradle of human applause to facing the frowns of an unfriendly world. They are frightened at the approach of persecution, and weep in discouragement, when they should be shouting praises over anticipated triumphs. Though sometimes showing more than infant powers, yet much time is spent by them with the prophet under the juniper tree, in babylike sobbings over fancied ills. Jesus called his disciples "babes" in this stage of their spiritual life, and many of their deeds proved the fitness of the title; but they soon got beyond it, and, girded with divine power, were spiritual giants. It is a blessed thing to be even a babe in Christ Jesus, for that means life and wonderful possibilities; but to remain one too long is to be a "dwarf."

In this section of Israel's journey they were spiritual cowards. They were permitted to engage in but one battle, and then conquered more through Moses' intercession than their own inborn bravery. So with many in the parallel religious life. They may be brave to face material batteries and bullets, but will cower before spiritual foes.

Some of them tremble beneath the triumphs of the tobacco devil, and wilt like Peter when questioned closely as to their religions affinities, in critical places. They are sometimes "afraid to speak," or "pray," or "plead" with sinners, and while the shouts of a defiant physical foe would but inspire their courage, they tremble at the sound of their own voices when raised in Jesus' name.

They hate this weakness; fight, and sometimes rise above it, and persist in duty despite the fears it brings. They have heard of a "perfect love" that casts out such soul-hindering and harassing fears, and for this they long and look, and soon with joy receive.

The people in this stage of their experience received the Law from without, not from within. So with Christians who have not entered into the Canaan of a Holy Ghost experience. It is only then that the promise is fulfilled which says, "I will put my laws in their minds, and write them in their *hearts.*" In spiritual Egypt the law of God is "hated" in the heart; in the saved wilderness experience, it is feared and kept; in the Canaan experience, it is loved and delighted in. In which are you?

In this stage they met the Amalekites, and put them to flight, but did not destroy them. What the Amalekites were to them, "inbred sin" — mentioned in Scripture as the "carnal mind," "body of death," and the "old man" is to the believer who is still out of the spiritual Canaan. Its presence within may be detected by various uprisings; such as pride, envy, selfishness, impatience, and sinful anger. These, like the Amalekites, may be so put to rout that none but God and self will be aware of their existence; but self is painfully conscious of it, and it brings bitterness and sadness of heart.

But one objects, "If inbred sin remains after conversion, then God at that time did not do a perfect work." With just as much sense might it be said, "If Israel had Amalek to fight afterward, then God did not effect a perfect deliverance at the Red Sea." Then he wrought for them a complete deliverance from Pharaoh and his service. And in a like manner at conversion he grants complete deliverance from the penalty of all past sins and imparts life eternal.

If at once the soul would feel its need, meet the conditions, and claim the cleansing, inbred sin would *at that time* be extirpated, and the soul pass into Canaan without any intervening wilderness experience. If you have done so, thank God, and pray for and sympathize with the multitudes not so highly favored.

The apostles had been for years with Jesus, knew that their "names were written in heaven," and in a restricted sense were "clean through the word which he had spoken;" but the inbred bent to evil which was manifested in their cowardice at critical times, their ambition and checkered experience, was eliminated only after passing through the "upper room" experience into Canaan. Isaiah evidently was a pardoned man and a prophet, but cleansed from inbred sin only after the "live coal" purgation.

That months, weeks, or *moments* need intervene between the two experiences, if the soul knows its privilege, is not needful; but that such is the usual experience of Christians, none who have made the matter a study will be foolish enough to deny. Some, on the discovery of this sinful tendency within thorn after conversion, being unenlightened as to its real nature and their privilege, give way to discouragement, and go back to Egypt. Others have said, "I'll kill it with good works," and foolishly have put them instead of Jesus' blood. Fletcher for a time belonged to this class.

Some have said, "Victory over inbred sin is to be gotten by growth," and they have grown in knowledge of themselves and of the Word; but inbred sin, like a cancer on a growing child, or like weeds by the side of growing flowers, has grown faster still, and smiles at their slowness to perceive the divine remedy.

Others reason, "Its presence is needful to keep us humble;" and, deceived by this device of Satan, cherish it as wisely as a man would roll in the mud to keep clean. Others have been deceived by the plea that we need it to contend with in order to gain the "overcoming" strength. As if the "world, the flesh, and the devil" were not enough to test and develop all our powers, without our being hampered by this treacherous bosom foe. Others say, "I'll keep it down;" but, instead, it often keeps them down. By and by the soul, sick of fruitless efforts, seeks a better way.

As God promised Israel that he would "*utterly put out the remembrance of Amalek from under heaven*," so has he promised to cleanse his children "from *all* unrighteousness," and utterly *destroy* the "body" of inbred sin, so that, the "old man" being "crucified" and "dead," the soul "purified by faith" and cleansed from "all its guilty stains," exults in blood-bought freedom, not from temptation or liability to sin, but from inborn carnality.

Let everything that hath breath praise the Lord for this freely proffered freedom from this insidious foe! an internal foe that has betrayed multitudes of spiritual Troys into the hands of the enemy; a "fire in the rear" foe, more subtle than any outside enemy; a foe that has betrayed into thousands of words and acts that have caused deepest pain to both God and man; a strongly entrenched foe, that none but divine artillery can dislodge.

It was the consciousness of the presence of this foe that led Dr. Levy in this stage of his experience to declare:

> I have experienced the blessing of justification; by it I have been absolved from all my past sins; by it I stand in the righteousness of Christ, and every privilege of a child of God, and every grace of the blessed Holy Spirit has been secured me; but I do not realize that it has destroyed the power of inbred sin or ended "the war in my members," or brought to me complete rest of soul. I have peace, but it is often broken by "fear which has torment." I am conscious of loving God, but like some sickly, flickering flame ... The ordinances of religion yield comfort and strength; but I find as often that all spirituality and power have retreated from them, leaving their channels dry.

Referring to this part of his life, Bishop Foster witnessed:

> Now I seemed again, as with the pressure of an invisible hand, forcibly conducted into the innermost chamber of my heart, and cherished sins and inward corruptions were revealed to me. How vile I seemed to be! What defilement filled my whole soul as a mantle! What a disparity between me and what a minister of Jesus ought to be! Never did I see inbred corruption in such a light before.

In spiritual Egypt inbred sin reigns; in the Sinai Wilderness it is stunned and chained; but in spiritual Canaan it is exterminated. With hastening feet let us press forward and cross the border line.

> *O, that I might at once go up,*
> *No more on this side Jordan stop,*
> *But now the land possess!*
> *This moment end my legal years,*
> *Sorrow and sins, and doubts and fears,*
> *A howling wilderness!*

5

Kadesh Barnea, the Believer's Waterloo

Prelude

YEA, THEY DESPISED THE pleasant land, they believed not his word: but murmured in their tents, and hearkened not unto the voice of the Lord. — Psalms 106:24, 25.

Harden not your heart, as in the provocation, in the day of temptation in the wilderness: when your fathers tempted me, proved me, and saw my works forty years ... Take heed, brethren, lest there be in any of you an evil heart of unbelief, in departing from the living God ... So we see that they could not enter in because of unbelief. —Heb. 3:8, 9, 12, 19.

> And I have wounded thee — O, wounded thee!
>> Wounded the dear, dear hand that holds me fast!
> O, to recall the word! that cannot be!
>> O, to unthink the thought that out of reach hath passed!
> Sorrow and bitter grief replace my bliss;
>> I could not wish that any joy should be;
> There is no room for any thought but this,
>> That I have sinned, have sinned — have wounded thee!
> How could I grieve thee so? Thou couldst have kept,
>> My fall was not the failure of thy word.
> Thy promise hath no flaw, no dire except
>> To neutralize the grace so royally conferred.

Kadesh Barnea, the Believer's Waterloo

PLACE: KADESH BARNEA. Many of the events occurring here are illustrative of those which occur in the lives of people when they come to the point of decision, and refuse to meet the conditions upon which the fullness of the Spirit's cleansing and keeping power is offered.

The children of Israel were conscious that they were on the border of Canaan. God said to them here, "Go in and possess the land," and promised them its rich possessions. Here, also, they listened to the report of those who had been sent to spy out the land. God's people reach a parallel experience where divine commands and promises, and the testimonies of those within the land of perfect love, all combine to convince them that they are upon its very verge.

Kadesh was the scene of Israel's defeat. It was the Waterloo of that unbelieving nation. Thousands have met their spiritual Waterloo in a parallel place in their religious life. The "bugbears" that here frightened them from Canaan have their counterpart in hindrances to holiness among believers now. Here believers, like the children of Israel at Kadesh, are confronted by defiant and boastful giants, which, if feared, will conquer; if faced, will fall. Some of them will be noticed.

1. *Giant Ignorance.* He seeks to shut out all knowledge of the goodly land, and will not scruple to use any means to accomplish his design. He tells his victims that the "wilderness" life is "good enough for this world," and has a trumpet with which he makes them deaf to God's commands and promises, and the testimony of his people as to the easy access into the "land of corn and wine." He also induces them to view the "walled towns" and "giants" with a mighty magnifying glass, and God's provision for their victory with one that minifies even more mightily. He hugely enjoys his tricks, and laughs as the people are "destroyed for lack of knowledge."

2. *Giant Prejudice.* He is a brother to the one just mentioned, and they work on nearly the same line. He succeeds by inducing whom he can to wear spectacles of his manufacture, through which the realities of a Canaan experience look distorted and repellent. Those victimized by him are sometimes heard to say, "I don't like the word sanctification; I don't believe in instantaneous and complete cleansing after conversion, and "I am prejudiced against professing holiness as a distinct blessing."

Many have felt like Bishop Foster, who, referring to the time when he was under the influence of this giant, said, "My mind was perplexed and confused, and filled with prejudice, not against holiness itself, but against its profession, and particularly by myself." Prejudice has thus deceived many, and then jeered at the queer antics they have cut while lingering on the borders of the land, or staggering backward into the wilderness of sourness, doubt, and despair. It is under the deceptions of these two giants that "peculiar personal views" of holiness and its attainment, contrary to the teachings of both the Church and the Word, have been held to the ruin of the soul.

3. *Giant Peculiar Circumstances.* His victims say, "My circumstances are so peculiar that it is an utter impossibility for me now to claim the blessing." In view of the manifold declarations of the Gospel as to its application to all of the needs of every believer, it would be thought that the success of this giant would be very limited; but, notwithstanding, he frightens thousands from the land.

A man called at the parsonage one day, and said that he felt it his duty and privilege to enter the land, but his peculiar circumstances forbade it at that time. "The truth is," he said, "my wife is a very nervous woman, and sometimes uses abusive language, and in order to keep her any-where in bounds I sometimes have to talk back in a way that would not be consistent with such a life." Before leaving he was led to see this trick of the giant, and entered Canaan. The next time I saw him I asked him how he got along with his wife and the new life. "O," he said, "all right. I guess the fault was as much mine as hers."

4. *Giant Legality.* He seeks to lure into the belief that entire sanctification is "of works," and not "of faith." Many, under the delusive spell this giant has thrown over them, have had to confess like one who afterward became a mighty soulsaver: "I bow my head in shame, and confess to him and to you that in my inmost soul I am sorry that I stayed away distrusting Christ, but studying books, studying the Bible, and doing every thing I could but the one thing that would have brought the blessing to my poor heart."

5. *Giant Formality.* He is a twin brother of Legality, and seeks to defeat in a kindred way.

6. *Giant Inbred sin.* He was crippled and put in chains at conversion, but at this point appears in strength to dispute further progress. He de-clares himself unconquerable by any power short of death, and mocks the idea of his being subject to extermination, even by Power Divine. Pride, Envy, Petulance, Temper, Selfishness, Unholy Ambition, and Fear are his children, and join their father in his defiance of any power to effect their ruin. By their braggadocio thousands have been put to flight.

7. *Giant Ecclesiasticism.* He is a very friendly appearing personage, belongs to the Church, is a class-leader of the class which "has a name to live, but is dead," and were it not for his affected manner and tone would

be taken for a friend instead of a foe. He seeks to frighten from the experience of perfect love by saying: "Many of the prominent Church members do not enjoy this blessing, and some of them are skeptical in regard to it. Your pastor does not preach it specifically, or even profess it. Do you aspire to be wiser or better than they?" If his victim is unfortunate enough to belong to a denomination that discounts the doctrine, he will make the most of that. A prominent Baptist clergyman, alluding to the time that this giant came well-nigh keeping him from the blessing, said, "The enemy brought before me, with tremendous force, my life-long prejudices, my theological training, my professional standing, my denominational pride. The dread of being misunderstood, of having my motives questioned, of being called 'unsound in doctrine,' of being slighted by my ministerial brethren, and treated with suspicion and coldness, filled my heart with unspeakable anguish." Beware of the sanctimonious sophistries of Giant Ecclesiasticism!

8. *Giant Egotism.* Those defeated because of the vauntings of this giant are heard to mutter: "I don't think as the Church teaches as to this matter;" "I've my own peculiar views;" "I can't take so much for granted as some folks;" and kindred ejaculations. If they only were as foolish as Finney, Wesley, Fletcher, Paul, and like people, who could "take so much for granted," they might condescend to cross over and possess the land; but, puffed up by Egotism, they perish in the wilderness.

9. *Giant Worldly Conformity.* Possessed of mighty strength, this giant seeks both to frighten and to bribe. He says, "What will people think of you if you live a life so different from many professors and from the world around you?" and threatens to crush with the weight of public opinion if the forward step be taken. He bribes by saying, "Accept my warnings, and all that worldlings prize most dear I will bequeath you."

Beneath his bribes and threats many a victim at this point has feared and failed to break with secular and secret societies, whose Christless and worldly nature has made it an impossibility to act therein and at the same time to live a holy life. "My Masonry must go," said a minister seeking holiness, to a prominent worker. It did not go, and he did not get the blessing. Giant Worldly Conformity counts him among his hosts of victims. Beware of both the giant's bluster and his bribes.

10. *Giant Black Habit.* At this point he often appears in full strength, to dispute further progress. He drugs some of his subjects with narcotics, and brutalizes others by tobacco and other stimulants, until they seem to nearly lose their senses; and then, when they desire to cross the line and enter Canaan, he shouts triumphantly, "You cannot stay there and keep me with you; *and I won't give you up.* Ha! ha! ha!" His laugh often keeps them from the land.

11. *Giantess Pride.* She is as mighty as any of her brethren, and even more ironical than they. She sneeringly says, "So you think of being holy, do you? Well, go on; throw off your worldly adornments; conform to the teachings of the Bible and your Church vows; give away your money for religious purposes, and be a target, if you want to, for the criticisms of your family and "*society!*"

She emphasizes the word "society" because she has reigned queen therein so long that she feels sure that none dare break its bonds or bear its censures. She dares the seeker to make the humble confessions upon which his victory hinges, and haughtily sneers at the "reproach of Christ." She has power to impart a kind of spiritual rheumatism, that affects the whole body from the knees to the neck, so that persons "cannot bear" to kneel in public prayer, and often "dread" to even bow the head. Her cheeks are flushed with success; for she has frightened untold numbers from the "promised land," has robbed God's treasury of millions of dollars with which to uniform her victims, and has led multitudes to sacrifice friends, honor, virtue, and life itself, at her bidding.

12. *Giant Indefiniteness.* This giant tries to prevail upon people to substitute an indefinite experience for perfect love, and then to expect it at an indefinite time, and seek it in an indefinite way. His victims are often "prejudiced" against the words "sanctification" and "perfect love," are afraid of making a "hobby of holiness," and instead do make a "hobby" of "a deeper work of grace," "more religion," and kindred indefinite phrases, which do not take them into the "promised land."

They are duped by Giant Indefiniteness, who laughs at their mortification as the fire and water of their "hobby engine" fails long before they reach the land, and is pleased at their perplexity as they behold the "holiness hobby" train steam gaily past them with its freight of joyous passengers, who reach their destination in the land on the King's time to the very minute.

13. *Giant Gratification*. He takes this name in this place because his true cognomen is too unseemly to mention here. He preys upon his victims in solitude. Multitudes of both sexes have been well-nigh ruined in body and in soul by his ravages. He was renounced at conversion, but, it may be, has ever since struggled for the mastery. At this point, with some, he arises in all his might and declares his defeat impossible. In God's strength he may be conquered, but if met without inflexible resistance he will drive the soul into the wilderness, and shout for joy over its bitter wail of despair.

14. *Giant Presumption*. He attempts to keep from the "land" by persuading people that they are in it when they are not. His victims present a pitiable spectacle; their lips professing holiness, and their lives belying it.

15. *Giant Emotion*. This Giant attempts to foil by persuading his victims that they must have the witness of the Spirit that they are in the land before they believe they are there. He blinds their eyes to the fact that their part is, first, complete submission; and then, second, complete trust in *God's Word*, and that God's part is to lead into the land; and third, to give the witness, and that his part is conditioned upon the performance of theirs, and always follows and never precedes it. He fools them into clamoring for the health and "good-feeling" of full salvation before they have taken the medicine of complete submission and trust.

16. *Giant Deception*. Referring to the time when he was quailing beneath the lies of this deceiver, Alfred Cookman wrote:

> Frequently I felt to yield myself to God, and pray for the grace of entire sanctification; but then this experience would lift itself in my view as a mountain of glory, and I would say, "It is not for me." I could not possibly scale that shining summit; and if I could, my besetments and trials were such I could not successfully maintain so lofty a position.

Though thus baffled for a little time, yet, through the aid of Bishop Hamline and his devoted wife, he soon put this giant to flight and triumphantly entered the land. When this giant cannot deceive in this way, then he often says, "The duties in the land will be so many and so severe that you never can do them;" and he makes a desperate effort to conceal the fact that entire sanctification does not impose one single new duty, but simply gives power and love to *cheerfully* do the duties devolving in a justified state; that it is simply throwing overboard all useless baggage, and claiming steampower to move the train to which the engine is already attached.

17. *Giant Bombast.* He struts up and down before his victims, shaking his fist at them, and brandishing his sword, until they are stupefied with terror. Then they, forgetting about God, his power and his promises, sometimes whisper to each other: "Should we enter the land we could not hold it, but would soon be driven out." Often, in their fright, they almost lose their reason, and sometimes say, "We surely dare not profess to be pure in heart and filled with the Holy Spirit, because then so much would be expected of us."

They would lift up their hands in holy horror should they hear any one say, "I don't dare to profess to be perfectly honest, lest people will expect too much of me;" or, "I don't profess to be perfectly virtuous, lest too much should be expected of me;" yet, in their fear-frenzy, they talk just as absurdly in regard to professing perfect loyalty to God. If they only would muster courage to give this giant one blow with the "Sword of the Spirit," he would vanish like a bubble. As it is, he frequently frightens his victims "to death." Under the influence of the giant's power, one who afterward became a possessor of perfect love and a bishop in our Church declared: "If my enjoyment of it requires a profession, I do not desire it. I do not feel that I could receive it on such terms or with such involvements."

18. *Giant stubbornness.* He seeks to prevail upon the soul to cling to some "idol" that the king will not permit to enter the land. He is among the mightiest to be resisted, and will slay, if not defeated.

19. *Giant Perverted Scripture.* He tears texts of Scripture from their places, and gives them meanings God never meant, contrary to both the context and whole scope of Holy Writ. Because it is impossible for mortals on earth to attain unto "absolute," "angelic," or "resurrection perfection," he would nullify all the commands and promises of Scripture in regard to "perfection in love," and make his dupes believe that that is also unattainable. He takes Paul's statement that he has not yet attained unto "resurrection perfection," and with it blindfolds their eyes to the fact of his profession of "Christian perfection." Because there is a sense in which "there is no man that sinneth not," and in which "if we say we have no sin we deceive ourselves, the truth is not in us," he takes these texts, and with them stops the ears of those whom he seeks to deceive to the sound of the manifold texts and testimonies of Scripture that declare,

in tones like the "voice of many waters," the privilege of being "made free from sin" — yea, even "dead unto sin, and alive unto God;" so that it is felt that even

> *The freedom from all willful sin,*
> *The Christian's daily task:*
> *O, these are graces far below*
> *What longing love would ask!*

He further tries to make them believe that, because the Bible declares that in one period of earth's history God looked down on the earth and "could not find one righteous man; no, not one," that there never can be one. He blinds them to the fact that it would be just as wise to reason that, because there was a time when no one could be found who believed in the earth's rotundity, therefore there never could or would be any such, and that the world is flat! With many kindred sophistries this giant has kept many from the land. He met Jesus in the wilderness, and never hesitates to wrest Scripture to the destruction of whomsoever he can. He is uniformed in a robe of light, but his heart is black with deception.

20. *Giant Unbelief.* He is commander-in-chief of the "giant legion," and is continually straining all his power to invent and execute new expedients for keeping his victims from the realms of perfect love. He is procurer for Giant Despair, of *Pilgrim's Progress* fame, and most of those vanquished by him die in Doubting Castle.

All of the giants threatening Israel at Kadesh were of heathen extraction. So all of those just mentioned, who seek to frighten from a holy life, are born of Satan and a corrupt heart. Israel was frightened by the bluster of the giants, and fled without even trying to conquer them. Many at spiritual Kadesh, in their "battle with the giants," have fled in a like cowardly way. Too late they have seen that the mightiest of these "giants" were but Satan's "scarecrows," bolstered up to keep them from the "goodly land."

May each reader, instead of following in the footsteps of defeated Israel, adopt the God-honoring, giant-defying report of Caleb and Joshua: "Let us go up at once and possess it; for we are well able to overcome it!"

6

Desert Wilderness Experience: Wretched Religion

Prelude

FOR THE CHILDREN OF Israel walked forty years in the wilderness, till all the people that were men of war, which came out of Egypt, were consumed, because they obeyed not the voice of the Lord; unto whom the Lord sware that he would not shew them the land, which the Lord sware unto their fathers that he would give us, a land that floweth with milk and honey. — Josh. 5:6.

But they rebelled and vexed his Holy Spirit; therefore he was turned to be their enemy, and he fought against them. — Isa. 63:10.

With many of them God was not well pleased: for they were overthrown in the wilderness. — 1 Cor. 10:5.

Let us therefore fear, lest, a promise being left us of entering into his rest, any of you should seem to come short of it. — Heb. 4:1.

> When we close our eyes to light,
> > Then how dark the dismal night!
> When our feet will not obey,
> > Then how thorny is the way!
> If God's promises we spurn,
> > How we feel his anger burn!

Desert Wilderness Experience: Wretched Religion

PLACE: "THE WILDERNESS." The events occurring in Israel's history here present a vivid picture of the *life of the backslider*. Some have vainly supposed "the wilderness" to be a picture of a justified life. Concerning this Dr. Pentecost says,

> We often hear it said that the Christian's life in this world corresponds to the life of the Children of Israel in the wilderness; and those wilderness wanderings are

often appealed to, to justify the uneven, crooked ways of Christians. Being overcome by sin day by day, it is said, "O, you know that we are in the wilderness now! By and by, when we get to heaven, we shall not be overcome." In a word, the type of the Christian's life on earth; and the promised land is made a type of heaven. But this is wide of the truth. Canaan is the type of the life which a Christian, under the captaincy of Jesus, our Heavenly Joshua, ought to lead down here. Israel in the land of promise shows us the Christian's life of victorious faith over "the world, the flesh, and the devil!"

Let the idea that this "Desert Wilderness" life is a type of any degree of genuine Christianity be buried in some secluded place, and on its gravestone write, "DIED FOR WANT OF SUPPORT."

I believe, however, that God has hung this photograph of a backslider in the gallery of his Word, that by its awfulness we might be warned of the perils of such a life. Let us study it, and be warned by it as we will wish we had when we come to die and stand before the great white throne!

1. *Israel did not backslide into the Sinai Wilderness experience*; nor does the believer who has received the light of a full salvation, and refused to walk in it, go back to the same life. He loses at this point his justification.

2. *Israel wept when it was too late.* When they realized the awful doom their unbelief had brought upon them, it is written that they "lifted up their voice, and cried, and the people wept that night." The same is true of those who reject perfect love; they weep, but when it is too late.

3. *They attempted to enter the land in their own time and way, and were repulsed.* "The Amalekites came down and smote them." Many who have felt that God's conditions of entering the "land" were "too strict," or that his time was not "convenient," like Israel, desiring the blessings of the land, have made a like fatal mistake, and the Amalekites and Canaanites of inbred sin have soon "discomfited" them. The lightning of divine disapproval ever leaps upon all compromises that men seek to substitute instead of obedience to God's commands.

4. *They were no longer divinely led.* There is evidence that the "pillar of cloud and of fire" was now withdrawn. In a like manner, every one who will not "follow Jesus" forfeits divine guidance. They "rejected his counsels," and he "laughed at their calamity," and "mocked" when their fear came. In a like manner the backslider in heart or life, "self-mystified" and "muddled up" as to Christian privilege, often feels himself a fit subject for just and divine ridicule.

5. *They became a nation of grumblers.* They "murmured against Moses and against Aaron," whom God had appointed to lead them, and against God himself. The same trait is prominent in their brethren of "wilderness" experience in the nineteenth century. They grumble. An old quatrain, changed a little, describes them:

> *From morning till night it is their delight*
> *To grumble away without stopping;*
> *Nor is there a day but they grumble away,*
> *Like water that's constantly dropping.*

They grumble about the preacher. He preaches too low or too loud, too long or too short, too slow or too fast; he visits too little or too much, and he is too jovial or too sad. They grumble about the brethren, the Church, their Church paper, the Discipline, their children, companions, crops, the weather, and God's providential dealings with them. They sometimes almost make home a hell for their family, and then, when God in mercy takes one of the household to himself, they grumble about that. Like their brethren in the days of the Son of Man, if John comes "neither eating bread nor drinking wine," they say, "He hath a devil." If Jesus comes "eating and drinking," they say, "Behold a gluttonous man and a winebibber, a friend of publicans and sinners!" Indeed, their sole song is:

> *Grumble, grumble, grumble,*
> *Grumble, grumble, grumble.*

This complaining state of soul is positive proof that its possessor has never been converted, or else is a wayward wanderer in the "Desert Wilderness."

6. *They maintained the form of piety without its power.* Their brethren in the spiritual "wilderness" often do likewise. The Jewish Church in the days of Jesus and the dead memberships of today are examples. People may pray, read the Bible, give, and attend worship, as strictly as the condemned Pharisee of old, and with as little profit to themselves and others. Like the dead tree, they have the body, branches, and perhaps the leaves, *but are destitute of life.* They have come up to a point where they

have rebelled, and forsaken God and substituted formality in his stead. The devil seeks to lull them into the belief that all yet may end well, and succeeds so well that many refuse to realize their awful condition until they are awakened in a dying hour, or in the eternal world, by the shrieks of the damned and the surgings of the fire-tossed sea.

7. *They sought to take the reins of government from the hands of God and control matters themselves.* They said, "Let us make a captain and return into Egypt." A like disposition exists today among the dwellers in the "wilderness." If ministers whom God has sent do not "please" them they seek those who will. If their ministers, as Wesley advised, "press believers to expect full salvation now," they will long for others who will "give them a little rest on that subject," and who will "please them," and perhaps lead them worldward.

A Church government that leaves the appointing power under God in the hands of earnest, praying men, becomes odious to such; and they have been known to band together in an organization, and call themselves a Church, and put the control of the pulpit in the hands of backsliders and other unconverted people. Such proceedings are a burlesque on Christianity, and are born of heart-badness.

8. *The children of Israel blamed others for the misery they brought upon themselves.* They blamed both God and his servants. Backsliders now are often guilty of a similar meanness. They trace their failure and consequent misery to the neglect of pastor or members, or some other source outside of themselves. Their sin is like that of a man who would set his house on fire, and then blame the carpenter who built the house or the company who manufactured the matches.

9. *They turned Egyptward.* "Let us ... return into Egypt." They had rejected their offered heavenly heritage, and hence their longings for the land of their servitude. When Christians refuse to "walk in the light," their souls soon sigh for the darkness. Thousands have reached the borders of the land of perfect love, but, refusing to enter, have soon been found sinking amid the swamps of sin, or perishing on the barren hillsides of unbelief which are numerous in the "wilderness" of woe.

They are far from the kingdom, and far from the crown—
From Christ and his ransoming cross;

> *O, infinite sadness! no eyes but his own*
> *Could weep such a fathomless loss.*

10. *They made crooked paths.* In wilderness experience No. 1, they followed the pillar of cloud and of fire; but having deserted that, and rejected divine guidance, they followed where fancy or fear might suggest, and their journey was a zigzag course, like the lives of those in all ages who have refused to follow the leadings of God's Spirit and his Word. Such, if they witness at all, will testify something as follows: "I know I do many things I ought not, and leave undone many things that I ought to do, and make many crooked paths; but I hope to continue and finally outride the storms of this unfriendly world, and land my soul on the fair banks of eternal deliverance." They seem blinded to the fact that, according to that testimony, they are out-and-out sinners, and that unless they repent and get justified, they will surely be lost forever!

Some of this class act as if they expect "good hopes," "good desires," or "good resolutions" to stand them instead of obedience to Jesus; but their delusion will be eternally dispelled when they hear him declare that none "but he that doeth the will of my Father" shall enter the eternal city. If they sing at all it is such words as

> *What peaceful hours I once enjoyed,*
> *How sweet their memory still!*
> *But they have left an aching void*
> *The world can never fill.*

Or —

> *In vain we tune our formal songs;*
> *In vain we try to rise;*
> *Hosannas languish on our tongues,*
> *And our devotion dies.*

How truly the above language paints their experience; yet what a sad spectacle! Sometimes in their perplexity, they give expression to their doubts by trying to sing—

> *'Tis a point I long to know*
> *Oft it causeth anxious doubt—*

Do I love the Lord or no?
Am I his or am I not?

God knows they are not; Satan knows they are not; good men and bad men often know they are not; and they seem to be the only beings in whose mind there lingers any doubt on the subject; and death and judgment soon will make it clear to them.

O, the horrors of "crooked-path" religion! It is to its votaries what the "blind staggers" is to the animal affected by it; it gets into much trouble and finally ends in death.

God says of them: "As for such as turn aside unto their crooked ways, the Lord shall lead them forth with the workers of iniquity." (Psa. 125:5.)

In the Sinai Wilderness experience the people were going the right way, and walked in a straight path, although often heavily burdened and sometimes falling down, quickly to arise again. In Canaan they "run and do not weary," for they are freed from their weights and borne up by power divine. In Egypt and the Desert Wilderness experience, they are going the wrong way, and stumble downward amid many foot-pits and "crooked paths." Angels weep over them, but devils shout with hellish glee.

11. *In the "desert" God's service became irksome.* Discontent dwelt in their hearts, and submission and peace were driven far away. The same is true in the parallel experience. An impulse soon comes to many to "leave the Church," "resign their positions," and to complain that the preaching is "too close" and the Bible way "too strict." A prominent worker describes his feelings, when snared in this woeful wilderness experience, as follows: "I became very much discontented with my position in the Church; the ministry became a burden to me; I became complaining, and anxious to retire, resolved to avail myself of the first opportunity to become a local preacher. I became at last completely wretched—more a slave than a child. It was manifest to me that in this way I could not live." Such are some of the testimonies that come from this "sepulchral wilderness."

12. *Their defeat encouraged the enemies of Israel.* In a like way the life of a backslidden man or Church strengthens the powers of darkness, and thus awakens shouts of derision from Satan and all his hosts.

13. *"And Israel joined himself unto Baal-peor, and the anger of the Lord was kindled against Israel."* First God was forsaken, and then Satan was

embraced. This illustrates one of the marked features of the "backslider's" life. He renounces the great "fountain of living waters," and then seeks "cisterns that can hold no water." Spiritualism, Universalism, Unitarianism, and kindred names stand simply for "broken cisterns."

Churches which "forsake God," in a like manner "join themselves to Baal-peor, and the anger of the Lord is kindled" against them. They forsake God by ignoring his presence and commandments and the conditions upon which he promises to "give the Holy Ghost." They "join themselves to Baal-peor" by pandering to the world.

(1) In adopting worldly schemes, such as "fairs," "festivals," "grab-bags," "masquerades," "crazy," "broom," "donkey," "snap and catch 'em," and similar sulfurous "socials," "quilt-*gambling*" projects, and kindred devices to support the gospel, instead of the God-given plan of systematic, proportionate giving by all, indicated in the inspired injunction, "Upon the first day of the week let every one of you lay by him in store as God has prospered him."

(2) In ignoring the God-revealed conditions of "grace in the heart," and putting the service of sacred song in the hands of people who are far from God. To put a sinner in the pulpit, so as to "get an influence over him and win him," were just as Scriptural as to make him a leader in song for that purpose. It were better to omit that part of the service than to go to "Baal-peor" for singers. When such things are practiced the "anger of the Lord is kindled;" and if persisted in, spiritual coldness and death will follow.

14. *The "wilderness" was worse than Egypt.* Some try to comfort themselves with the thought that, as the unbelieving never went back to Egypt, so all who are converted cannot go clear back to the Egypt of sin. They do not go there, but they do get in a worse condition. Egypt was a garden compared with the wilderness, and the horrors of the desert were doubly intensified by the fact that they had viewed the hills and vales and fruits of Canaan. So with the backslider. He has been made to feel that the ways of the world are wrong, and has "seen Jesus" in such a light that old pleasures and associations have ceased to charm, and the soul drops into the awful woe of the "backslider." God declares of such that their "latter end is worse than the beginning," and that "it had been better for them not to have known the way of righteousness, than, after they have known it, to turn from the holy commandment delivered unto them."

15. *The unbelieving Israelites perished in the wilderness and went to hell.* Some have vainly thought that, because they did not get back to Egypt, therefore they were saved, and that, in a like manner, all who ever have been converted can never be lost. "Once in grace, always in grace." The fallacy of such delusive reasoning is exposed by the divine reminder: "I will therefore put you in remembrance, though ye once knew this, how that the Lord, having saved the people out of the land of Egypt, afterwards destroyed them that believed not." (Jude 5.)

That the destruction here mentioned means the eternal doom of the damned is clear from the fact that, in the two following verses, it is connected with that of the angels "reserved in everlasting chains under darkness," and with that of Sodom and Gomorrah, which "are set forth for an example, suffering the vengeance of eternal fire." To live in the Desert Wilderness experience is to be inexpressibly miserable. To die there is to go to hell.

Moses, Caleb, Joshua, and many more, were compelled to suffer because of the sins of the others. Only the rebellious were forever lost, but others suffered by their sin. The analogy holds good in the parallel religious experience. Parents are pained because of the backslidings of children, and children are hampered because of the wanderings of parents; wives "sigh" for husbands who will live and die in the "wilderness;" and whole Churches languish because of the "desert" experiences of official members.

16. *God remembered Israel, even in the wilderness.* "Yea, forty years didst thou sustain them in the wilderness." He dealt kindly with them, and sought in many ways to win their love and allegiance. In a like manner deals he with the spiritual wanderer. He says, "How can I give you up?" and awaits in love to welcome the prodigal, and give him the best his house affords, so that, sin-sick wanderer in the "wilderness of woe," thou mayest even now say:

> *Though I forget him and wander away,*
> *Still he doth love me wherever I stray.*
> *Back to his dear, loving arms would I flee,*
> *When I remember that Jesus loves me.*

Remember that —

Softly and tenderly Jesus is calling,
 Calling for you and for me;
See on the portals he's waiting and watching,
 Watching for you and for me.

Why should we tarry when Jesus is pleading,
 Pleading for you and for me?
Why should we linger and heed not his mercies
 Mercies for you and for me?

Time is now fleeting, the moments are passing,
 Passing from you and from me;
Shadows are gathering, death-beds are coming,
 Coming for you and for me.

O for the wonderful love he has promised,
 Promised for you and for me!
Though we have sinned he has mercy and pardon,
 Pardon for you and for me.

Come home, come home;
 Ye who are weary, come home;
Earnestly, tenderly, Jesus is calling,
 Calling, O wand'rer, come home!

7

Entering Canaan

Prelude

T HEN J OSHUA COMMANDED THE officers of the people, saying, Pass through the host, and command the people, saying, Prepare you victuals; for within three days ye shall pass over this Jordan, to go in to possess the land, which the Lord your God giveth you to possess it ... And they answered Joshua, saying, All that thou commandest us we will do, and whithersoever thou sendest us we will go. — Josh. 1:10, 11, 16.

Having, therefore, brethren, boldness to enter into the holiest by the blood of Jesus, by a new and living way, which he hath consecrated for us, through the vail, that is to say, his flesh; and having a high priest over the house of God; let us draw near with a true heart in full assurance of faith, having our hearts sprinkled from an evil conscience and our bodies washed with pure water. — Heb. 10:19, 22.

> *When we follow Jesus' voice,*
> > *How our raptured hearts rejoice!*
> *When we yield to his control,*
> > *How our Jordans backward roll!*
> *When we welcome his command,*
> > *Then, how soon in Beulah land!*

Entering Canaan

PLACE: AT THE RIVER JORDAN. Theme: Crossing the river.

The events occurring here are illustrative of those which transpire when the believer, by complete consecration and trust, enters into spiritual Canaan.

1. *Israel had gained nothing by delay.* Their enemies had improved the forty years that had elapsed in strengthening their men and munitions to resist them; and, besides this, the river Jordan now lay between them and the "promised and." Delay of entering spiritual Canaan invites similar obstacles. The "giants" will grow stronger, and the "walled towns" be

more completely fortified, and some seemingly insuperable river will at last roll between the soul and the blessing.

2. *They had learned wisdom from God's judgments.* Their own sufferings and the awful deaths of the "unbelieving" in the wilderness had made them submissive. Thousands have been brought to entire consecration by like measures. There are those who will "learn righteousness" only "when God's judgments are in the earth." Sickness, disappointments, and bereavements, prove angels in disguise, and lead them from waywardness to the very borders of the "promised land."

3. *They were led into the land by a minister who enjoyed perfect love.* Moses' "mantle" fell upon Joshua, and he "followed fully," amid high tides of opposition, the counsels of his Lord. No minister is fitted to lead the people until be himself is "following fully." Unschooled men, "filled with the Spirit," have led thousands into the spiritual Canaan, while doctors of divinity without it have proved "blind leaders of the blind." Jesus' rule for this dispensation was, not to let a preacher, even though he had been with him for years, go out until he received the Pentecostal "diploma." Are we wiser than he?

4. *The Jordan consecration service was preceded by fitting preliminary instruction.* (See Joshua 1.) No better counsel for candidates seeking entire sanctification can be found than is here recorded.

(a) *They were here commanded to "go over,"* not *"grow over,"* and possess Canaan. So are we.

(b) *They were here reminded that Canaan was a "gift" land;* "the land that I do give them," said the Lord. Likewise the "love," "power," and the "Holy Spirit," which constitute the spiritual Canaan, are "gifts" of God, and are to be claimed without "money and without price."

(c) *They were here promised possessions:* "Every place that the sole of your foot shall tread upon, that have I given unto you;" power: "There shall not any man be able to stand before thee all the days of thy life;" and prosperity: "For then shalt thou make thy way prosperous, and then thou shalt have good success." Spiritual possessions, "incorruptible" and "fadeless;" spiritual "power over all the power of the enemy," and success such that "whatsoever he doeth shall prosper," are in a like manner offered to all who will be perfect in love.

What Joshua was to them the Holy Spirit is to the believer at spiritual Jordan. He explained God's messages, and directed them what to do in each exigency. The Spirit "takes the words of Jesus, and shows them unto us." We are to be "led by the Spirit;" and if in anything we be "otherwise minded, even this he shall reveal unto us."

5. *The source of their strength was to be the divine presence.* "I will not leave thee nor forsake thee." The same promise is given to all who will enter the spiritual Canaan. When the conditions upon which this promise is given are met, and its meaning realized and rested in, "giants" and "walled towns" shrink into nothingness.

6. *They were to be guided by the revealed Word.* "Thou shalt meditate therein day and night, that thou mayest observe to do according to all that is written therein." In entire consecration the believer in a like manner vows to be guided by the Word in all things.

7. *Israel, before taking the Canaan consecration pledge, was commanded to be very courageous.* "Be strong and of good courage," was the triply emphasized commandment. All who enter upon a life of complete loyalty to God need like counsel. Millions under its influence have felt and sung:

> *Sure I must fight if I would reign;*
> *Increase my courage, Lord!*
> *I'll bear the toil, endure the pain,*
> *Supported by thy Word.*

With the Master's "Be not afraid" sounding in their ears, they have hushed their fears, and boldly signed an eternal YES to all of God's requirements.

8. *Israel, at this point, made a complete consecration of all to God,* saying: "All that thou commandest us we will do, and whithersoever thou sendest us we will go." In a sense they had been consecrated ever since they broke away from Egypt; but now, in the light of all of God's commands and promises, of their past experience and hopes of future conquest, they make a specific and complete consecration. So with the believer when he obtains full salvation he yields all his powers to God for time and for eternity. Submission at conversion is like the surrender of the rebel and his oath of allegiance to the government, while the consecration made at the time of entire sanctification is more

like the enlistment of the soldier. Wrong ideas of what entire consecration really is have hindered some right at this point.

(a) *The idea that entire consecration and entire sanctification are identical.* A person may be entirely consecrated up to the point of acting faith in God's promises that would bring the blessing, but neglecting to do this, he would still stay outside the land. Entire consecration is man's part; entire "cleansing" and "filling" is God's. Entire consecration bears the same relation to these that a perfect engine does to the steam that will put it in motion and enable it to meet the end for which it was made.

(b) *Entire consecration is sometimes confounded with repentance.* Repentance is turning from the wrong way, putting down the brakes and reversing the engine. Entire consecration is submission of engine to any work the owner may wish. Entire sanctification is the engine, fired up, steam on, and in full motion. In God's Word sinners are commanded to "repent," but believers to "consecrate" or "yield themselves" unto God.

(c) *Others have imbibed the notion that in consecrating they were yielding something to God that did not previously belong to him.* Such need to remember that every power and possession of a human being is already God's by "creation, preservation, and redemption," and that when we "consecrate our all" we are simply "taking hands off from God's property," and acknowledging his right to his own. What would be thought of Mr. A., should he find a twenty dollar gold piece belonging to his employer in his possession, and, after a severe struggle over the matter, conclude to "consecrate" it to its owner? Yet many act just as stupidly in regard to that which belongs to their Maker.

(d) *It is also a mistake to suppose that consecration "as far as I know" is entire consecration.* "It must be as far as God knows." In the very nature of the case much must be subscribed to, that at the time cannot be known. It cannot be known how great our capacities will be, or what means may fall into our hands, or what God's Word and Spirit may reveal as duty, upon what errands he may wish to send us, or what crosses he may see fit to send; so, with Israel, we must cover all this ground with "whatsoever" and "wheresoever," and obediently trust our Father for the "what" and "where." How inexpressibly delicious to feel that

> *Where he may lead I'll follow,*
> *My trust in him repose,*

And every hour in perfect peace,
I'll sing, He knows, he knows!

The "as far as I know" consecration is as if one had the whole world to consecrate, and should take his station in the valley where but a fraction of his possession can be seen, and then consecrate as far "as he can see." He would not get the blessing. He ascends a hilltop, where his range of vision is broader, and repeats the consecration with like results. Then he scales a mountain summit, and then from one of earth's highest peaks, with a telescope, his vision sweeps a much wider circle, and he consecrates it all, but does not get the blessing. He has been consecrating "as far as he can see."

Finally, in despair, he bows before God and vows, "I yield all to thee— all that I can see, and all that is beyond my sight; the little that I am, and all I ever may be; this world as it is, and as it will be when all its resources are developed; and if in my name there are other worlds that I do not now know of; them, too, I yield to thee; and to all thy will as it is revealed, and as it may hereafter be made known, by thy assisting grace, I yield, *and will forever yield.*"

Thus the fully consecrated soul covenants to yield *all eternally to Jesus.* And the "all" includes every power of the being, as it is and as it will be when it has by use increased ten-fold, a million-fold. It includes all earthly goods now possessed, and all that will be when the undiscovered gold mine is developed, or the princely legacy received. It includes everything now made plain, and all that ever will be through the years of time and cycles of eternity. It includes all, not as measured by changing human vision, from the valley or hilltop or mountain; but as seen by the Omniscient Eye. This is what God meant when he said, "If we walk in the light *as he is in the light.*"

It is as if God should say, "My child, I have mapped out for you just the life-plan that you need; you can understand, and need to know but little of it now, but I will reveal it to you, explain it, and give you wisdom and strength to execute it as you need. Will you subscribe to it?" Complete consecration responds: "Blessed Lord, write out my orders and my discipline for this life and the life to come, and, by thy grace, I promise to say amen to every word."

Many things in the life that are not consistent with God's will may not arise at the moment the consecration is made, but as soon as they are seen they are made to harmonize. Some have foolishly reasoned as a certain brother did in regard to his tobacco. He made a complete consecration, exercised the faith, and crossed over into Canaan. He had been there but a short time when his tobacco habit confronted him. He reasoned: "God sanctified me with my tobacco; therefore it cannot be wrong to use it." But it still bothered him.

Then he prayed, "If using this is wrong, then, O God, take thy Holy Spirit from me." In an instant the Spirit took his flight, and the horrors of the darkness that followed, the brother never wishes again to feel. He cried out, "It is enough; I yield!" Tobacco went, the Spirit returned, and he again rejoiced in his presence, having learned the lesson that the fully consecrated soul should yield at once to all of the Spirit's corrections.

One asks, "But how can we know when all is consecrated?" Just as the soldier knows that he will execute the orders of his superior, or die trying to. Yes, even more surely, for man might require impossibilities; God cannot. Just as a person knows when he has deeded all his property to another, or promised a superior implicit obedience.

Israel at Jordan yielded the last point. The "whatsoever" and "wheresoever" covered the whole ground. I heard a minister's wife once say that, in reviewing her consecration, she always "ran up against something" that she was not willing to do. Too many are like her in this respect. This is the secret of its being "so hard" for many to believe.

If the Israelites at Jordan had held on to their tobacco, if they had had it, or their "jewelry" or "godless organizations," or had insisted on putting their music in the hands of the ungodly instead of the people divinely fitted for that work, or held to wrong means for raising money instead of bringing in their tithes, or retained unscriptural practices in their business, or in any other way "kept back a part of the price," they would have found it as difficult to exercise the "faith that brings the fire" as their brethren and sisters of today.

At Jordan, as at the Red Sea, the people were victorious through faith. Their surroundings differed, but in each instance it was *faith* that made them victorious. At the Red Sea they were threatened by enemies in the rear; here by foes in the van. In a like manner, at conversion it is the fury of the adversary and sins of the past that spur the seeker; while at entire sanctification it is the work in the van that calls for power from on high to do it.

At the Red Sea the waters were divided before they reached them; at Jordan their feet "touched the water's brim" before it receded. In a similar way faith is often tested more at the Jordan of cleansing and enduement than at the Red Sea of conversion.

At the Red Sea they exercised faith in God's specific promise to deliver them "out of Egypt;" at Jordan in his just as specific promise to lead them triumphantly "into Canaan."

At the Red Sea of conversion faith is exercised in God's promise to "pardon," and deliver "out of the hand of our enemies," and grant us "spiritual life." At the Jordan of cleansing and enduement our faith appropriates his oath-attested promise to "cleanse from all sin," "baptize with the Holy Ghost," and thus lead triumphantly "into spiritual Canaan," where we may "serve him without fear, in holiness and righteousness before him, all the days of our life."

In both instances it is the same "hand of faith" that is extended; but in the first instance it is reached out for pardon and sonship, and in the second for purity and power. In both instances the promises are pleaded; but in the first instance it is the promise of pardon and citizenship, while in the second it is for help to lay aside impediments, and claim armor, ammunition, and weapons, to fit for aggressive warfare.

In both instances the promises which faith appropriates are more reliable than any bank-paper earth ever saw; for they are the word of the Eternal, whose every promise is yea and amen in Christ Jesus, and who, "willing more abundantly to show unto the *heirs of promise* the immutability of his counsel, confirmed it by an oath; that by two immutable things, in which it was impossible for God to lie, *we might have a strong consolation*, who have fled for refuge to lay hold upon the hope set before us."

One says, "I don't doubt God's Word, but its application to my case." If you have not unreservedly yielded each and all points, of course you cannot claim its application; but if you have, do not hesitate for a moment to claim the promise that he receives and cleanses you. He says he does, and "he that believeth hath the witness in himself; *he that believeth not God maketh him a liar*, because he believeth not the record that God gave of his Son." "The record" is that "if we walk in the light, as he is in the light, we have fellowship one with another, *and the blood of Jesus Christ his Son cleanseth us from all sin.*"

The next step that the children of Israel took after making the entire consecration was to act accordingly. At God's command they arose, followed the "ark of testimony," and crossed the Jordan. In a like manner the believer, having fully yielded all to God, is to begin to put his bargain in practice, and, following the more "sure word of prophecy," "reckon himself to be dead indeed unto sin, and alive unto God."

At this point Israel appropriated the long-neglected promise of possessing Canaan, and triumphantly took possession. Israel's part was: 1. To yield fully to God; and 2. Trust him to give the victory. God's part was: 1. To lead them into the land as he had promised; 2. Make them conscious that they were there. His part of the contract was conditioned upon and followed the performance of their part. They met the conditions, stepped out on God's promise, and God met them, frightened their foes, rebuked Jordan even as he did the Red Sea, and in an instant they were in possession of the land. They believed it; they knew it.

In the parallel experience the same steps are to be taken. Man fully yields, and then in the present tense fully trust's God's promises of a spiritual Canaan on earth; and then God leads into the land and gives the witness of it. Then the soul begins to feel

> *'Tis so sweet to trust in Jesus,*
> *Just to take him at his word;*
> *Just to rest upon his promise;*
> *Just to know, 'Thus saith the Lord.'*

The first thing that Israel did after entering Canaan was to establish, by divine command, a memorial of the event. For this purpose they set up twelve stones: "And these stones shall be a memorial for the children of Israel forever." The Red Sea and Jordan marked two memorable events in their history, which they were commanded to explain to their children to all generations. In a like manner the Red Sea of conversion and the Jordan of entire sanctification should be commemorated by God's people. Ordinary birthdays and holidays should pale before them, like a tallow candle before the meridian sun. Other great blessings may have preceded these, and fallen between them, and certainly will follow them; but none so great as these. Blessed days! May their memories grow brighter forever!

8

Canaan: Spiritual Sunshine

Prelude

AND THEY TOOK STRONG cities, and a fat land, and possessed houses full of all goods, wells digged, vineyards, and olive yards, and fruit trees in abundance: so they did eat, and were filled and became fat, and delighted themselves in thy great goodness. — Neh. 9:25.

That ye might walk worthy of the Lord unto all pleasing, being fruitful in every good work, and increasing in the knowledge of God; strengthened with all might, according to his glorious power, unto all patience and longsuffering with joyfulness; giving thanks unto the Father, which hath made us meet to be partakers of the inheritance of the saints in light. — Col. 1:10-12.

> When we yield with all the heart,
> How our doubts and fears depart!
> When we fully trust the blood,
> How we sink beneath its flood!
> How it cleanses from all sin,
> Making pure and bright within!
> How each grace from heaven grows,
> When his Spirit Christ bestows!
> How the Spirit's fruits abound,
> When in Christ complete we're found!
> How his fullness satisfies
> All who dwell neath Beulah's skies!

Canaan: Spiritual Sunshine

THEY WERE IN CANAAN, and knew it. Both God and their surroundings declared it. The desert was behind, and vine-clad Canaan on either hand. In a like manner the entirely sanctified soul is made conscious of its condition by a consciousness begotten directly by God, and also by the "fruits of the Spirit," which will adorn the life as the vines the hills of Palestine.

The fact that they were in the land doubtless affected each person in a different way. One would weep, and another laugh. Some would shout, and others feel quiet. The same is true of those who enter the Beulah land of perfect love.

> One person realizes principally a marked increase of faith, and calls it the *"rest of faith."* Another is conscious of a deep, sweet resting in Christ, and he calls it *"resting in God."* Another is permeated with a sense of the divine presence, and filled with ecstatic rapture, and he calls it the *"fullness of God."* Another feels his heart subdued, melted, refined, and filled with God, and he calls it *"holiness."* Another realizes principally a river of sweet, holy love flowing through the soul, and he calls it *"perfect love."* Another is prostrated under the power of the refining, sin-killing Spirit, and he calls it *"the baptism of the Holy Ghost;"* and another realizes principally a heaven of sweetness in complete submission to God, and he calls it *"entire sanctification;"* while another may feel clearly and strongly conscious of complete conformity to all of the will of God, and calls it *"Christian perfection;"*

Or, as sometimes is the case, these different feelings may so blend and intertwine that he will rejoice in the consciousness of a mighty, soul-satisfying change, without stopping to name it. He *knows,* and *knows* that he *knows,* that his will is sweetly lost in his Heavenly Father's. Praise the Lord.

In Canaan they had battles to fight. Their Jerichos were to be taken, and enemies were continually seeking to dislodge them. In spiritual Canaan the same is true. Inbred sin is cleansed away, but natural appetites and impulses must be properly controlled, and the "world, the flesh, and the devil" still seek supremacy. Never this side of the grave do the saints reach an altitude where they can afford to stop singing

> *My soul, be on thy guard!*
> *Ten thousand foes arise;*
> *The hosts of sin are pressing hard,*
> *To draw thee from the skies.*

In the land of promise Israel needed to be very watchful. Let the believer learn from them. Jesus was tempted, and the servant never will get higher than his Lord. *"Watch* and pray!" shouts the great Captain of our salvation. To be deaf to this command is to dare infinite peril.

Israel was in danger of being driven from the land. They remained victors only by keeping intact the conditions upon which they entered.

"Wherefore let him that thinketh he standeth, take heed lest he fall." In spiritual Egypt and in the Desert Wilderness experience, like a hog in the mud, it is impossible to fall. In the Sinai Wilderness experience danger of falling is very great, because of the dim light and awful burden of inbred sin. In Canaan the danger still remains; but by the "marvelous light," the freedom from "carnality," and the perpetual presence of the Almighty "Keeper," it is comparatively small. If we will "remember" and keep hold of God's hand, we have his positive promise that he is able not only to "keep us from falling," but to present faultless before the throne of his glory, with exceeding joy." Hallelujah!

In Canaan Israel "grew" as a nation as never before. Perfect love is the tropics of spiritual growth. It is the "large place" that keeps enlarging, the "deep waters" that are ever deepening, the "bright light" that is ever brightening. Some have vainly thought that, because perfect love is received by faith, therefore, when obtained, growth ceases. Huge fallacy! A child with a cancer, confined to a dimly lighted room, will grow; but cure the disease, and let it leap into the sunshine and the pure air, and will growth cease? The converted man is the child of God, still diseased and in the shade. Entire sanctification is his complete cure and liberation. The spiritual Canaan experience that follows is the fresh air and sunshine in which he will "grow up" in value "like a cedar in Lebanon," in spiritual beauty like "the lily," and in righteousness like "an holy temple unto the Lord."

Canaan was higher up than Egypt. Some say, "O, we cannot expect to be always on the mountaintop." Such forget that the foot of Jesus' cross was on the top of Mount Calvary, and that the foot of our cross is high up on the summit of the mount of entire Trust and Consecration; and that hence to *keep at the foot of the cross is to abide on the top of the mountain.*

Israel was completely in the land, yet as a nation was not mature. With them, and with the believer, there is a vast difference between completeness and maturity. Complete cleansing and complete filling come by faith, and instantaneously; but maturity, with the complete saint as with the complete apple, is the child of growth and contact with ripening influences.

In the land of Canaan the people sometimes made mistakes. These were called "sins of ignorance," and provision was made for them. (See Levit. 4.) Believers sometimes make similar blunders. "If we say we have no sin [of ignorance], we deceive ourselves, and the truth is not in us." Jesus doubtless referred to them when he taught believers to pray, "Forgive us our trespasses." And in view of human liability to commit them, even in Canaan, we cannot omit that part of the prayer. But let it be remembered that there is just as much difference between the moral character of "sins of ignorance and "willful sin" as there is between the act of a man who aims at a tiger and unwittingly hits his child and the act of the intentional assassin.

The first flush of victory was followed by defeat and disappointment. The triumph at Jericho is followed by defeat at Ai. They had to learn that victory comes from implicitly minding and trusting God, and also that the treachery of one may bring a temporary defeat to many. How true in the parallel spiritual experience? How slow we are to learn that holiness consists, more than any thing else, in minding and trusting Jesus!

And how sad that modern Achans, who, like their ancient brother, think more of "gold" and "goodly garments" than of God's work and commandments, sometimes, in a like manner, bring temporary defeat to the Church and ruin to themselves! God's prompt disposal of him, and the victory that followed, teaches a lesson of the salutary influence of Church discipline in such cases.

What if they had said, "It will be so unpleasant to carry out the *Discipline*;" "You can't pull up the tares without destroying the wheat," and have left the matter for the next administration? The result would have been, as it is in similar instances now, an organization without power, without victory, and without God! Holy Ghost Churches, like Israel at Ai, will favor a firm exercise of godly discipline.

"As for the Jebusites the inhabitants of Jerusalem, the children of Judah could not drive them out; but the Jebusites dwell with the children of Judah at Jerusalem unto this day." (Josh. 15:63) What the Jebusites were to them, human Infirmities are to saints in Canaan. Inadvertance, Ignorance, Error, and Forgetfulness are their children, and with him are placed under tribute. Here they are to be borne with; in the heavenly Canaan they will be exterminated.

"I will take sickness away from you." (Ex. 23:25.) "And the Lord will take away from thee all sickness." (Dent.7:15.) Such were the gracious promises that God then made to his people. The promise was conditioned upon their keeping the strictest hygienic rules, and implicit obedience to and trust in God. That the passages apply in spiritual Canaan to

perfect health and strength of the spiritual nature none will deny. That they apply also, in many instances, to the body when *similar spiritual and sanitary conditions are met*, there can be no doubt.

It may be that these promises bring us to the borders of a world of privilege which has not been fully explored, and that we, in our eagerness to treasure the gold of spiritual good, have let many coppers of physical blessing fall to the ground. It surely seems as if provision for the body under the new dispensation cannot be less complete than under the old. And the New Testament promises, and examples of bodily healing, and the numberless reliable testimonies of its reality in all ages, prove beyond question that in many instances these promises apply to it.

"Thou shalt be blessed above all people; there shall not be male or female barren among you." (Deut. 7:14.) God is opposed to childless homes. He would rather work a miracle, as he did with Abraham and Zacharias, than have a home without children. What this promise was to them it doubtless is to all in spiritual Canaan, whom God has not called to some special work that forbids it. But, more than this, it is also to us a promise of spiritual children—

> *Better than daughters or than sons,*
> *Temples divine of living stones,*
> *Inscribed with Jesus' name.*

We shall "teach transgressors," and "sinners shall be converted." We shall "go forth weeping, and come again "rejoicing, bringing our sheaves."

In Canaan God's people were to be honest. "Thou shalt have a perfect and just weight, a perfect and just measure shalt thou have." Real possessors of perfect love would die rather than cheat. Before entering Canaan they were honest, now always cheerfully so. If they are employers they will "exact no more than is due," and cheerfully grant men their wages. If dealers, they will gladly give "good measure, pressed down and running over." If employees, they will cheerfully do all for their employers as for themselves, remembering that God's eye is upon them, and they "serve the Lord Christ." Holiness has sometimes been hindered by contemptible business "looseness" and "overreaching" in some of its professors. Such deeds prove their deception.

They were to keep their promises. "When thou vowest a vow unto the Lord, thou shalt not slack to pay it; for the Lord thy God surely will require it of thee; and it would be sin in thee." In spiritual Egypt and the Desert Wilderness men ignore their vows to God. In the Sinai Wilderness experience they pay them, though sometimes reluctantly. In spiritual Canaan they delight to do it. People sometimes act pious in other ways, when at the same time they are living in open violation of their "conversion," "baptism," "Church membership, "ministerial consecration," or other solemn vows which they have of their own freewill made unto the Most High. In God's sight they are "covenant-breakers." He awaits their tears of penitence and reformation, and is ready to lead them to a land of love, where a vow-keeping will be easy and sweet.

In Canaan they were to be cheerful givers. "Every man shall give as he is able, according to the blessing of the Lord thy God which he hath given thee." (Deut. 16:17.) To thus give becomes one of the most delightful exercises of all truly sanctified souls. To find that they were losing this spirit would frighten them as much as to detect in their hearts a disrelish for prayer, testimony, or pointed preaching. They feel it just as black a crime to withhold from God as to rob their fellowman. "God shovels in and they shovel out, and he is so much stronger than they that he always keeps ahead of them." Their *best* is given to God, and he gives them *his* best here, and promises to "withhold no good thing" from them throughout eternity. What a Father! Is it any wonder that the angels shouted "Glory to God in the highest!"

In Canaan they were to be humble. "Speak not thou in thine heart after that the Lord hath cast them out before thee, saying, For my righteousness the Lord hath brought me in to possess this land." Holy people are always humble. A perpetual edict against self-righteousness is proclaimed throughout the length and breadth of spiritual Canaan.

They were to make no compromises or enter into no alliances with the people of the land. "And ye shall make no league with the inhabitants of this land" (Judges 2:2);" Throw down their altars;" "Destroy their pictures and images;" "Pluck down their high places;" "Utterly overthrow them," and kindred commands were given them in regard to the enemies of God. In spiritual Canaan kindred commands prevail. We are to "come out from among them," "be separate," and "have no fellowship with the works of darkness." God frowns upon marriages with the ungodly, fellowship of saints with Christless organizations, and unholy business alliances. Souls have become entangled in such meshes, to regret it eternally. Worldly conformity in Church business and Church worship, and home business and home worship, are also prohibited by this principle. Indeed, in the entirely sanctified experience these alliances are loathed instead of loved.

In Canaan they were an holy people. "For I am the Lord your God: ye shall therefore sanctify yourselves, and ye shall be holy." (Levit. 11:44.) In the parallel spiritual experience God's people are "called not unto uncleanness, but holiness;" and "this is the will of God, even their sanctification." Holy agencies have brought them into a holy land, and by God's grace they have become a holy people. Christ, their altar, sanctifies them the sacrifice. Like Israel in Canaan, they have avouched the Lord to be their God, and to walk in his ways, and to keep his statutes and his commandments and his judgments, and to hearken unto his voice. (See Deut. 26:17-19.) "And the Lord hath avouched them to be his peculiar people, as he hath promised them, and that they shouldest keep all his commandments, and to make them high above all people that he hath made, in praise and in name and in honor, and that they may be a holy people unto the Lord their God, as he hath spoken." Hallelujah!

In Canaan they were to love God supremely. "And thou shalt love the Lord thy God with all thine heart, and with all thy soul, and with all thy might." (Deut. 6:5.) If they did this in the dim light of that day, how much more should we amid the dazzling splendors of this! In spiritual Canaan "love is the fulfilling of the law." All gifts and all other graces pale in its presence, and the soul feels

> *O glorious hope of perfect love!*
> *It lifts me up to things above;*
> *   It bears on eagles' wings;*
> *It gives my ravished soul a taste,*
> *And makes my soul forever feast*
> *   With Jesus, priests, and kings.*

It casts out fear, transforms duty to delight, and links saints of all sects inseparably to each other, to angels, and to God. It is its atmosphere that makes spiritual Canaan the Beulah (married) Land of the redeemed and the Redeemer.

They were to be obedient in all things. Their instructions were: "What thing soever I command you, observe to do it; thou shalt not add thereto or diminish from it." In spiritual Egypt we are openly disobedient; in a justified state we obey, although often protesting. In spiritual Canaan we "love his commandments," and "*delight* to do his will;" in an unconverted and backslidden state we walk in our own ways; in a converted state we "follow Jesus," although sometimes reluctantly and afar off; in a fully sanctified state we count it all joy to be with him and obey him always and everywhere. We do not even feel like "adding to" or "diminishing from" any commandment that we know to be of him.

> *Day by day we "fully follow,"*
>   *Where in love he leads,*
> *By his Spirit's loving counsels*
>   *Holding all our deeds;*
> *And yielding thus to his sweet will,*
> *Celestial joys our spirits fill.*

SWEET REST IN JESUS
Tune: "Rest for the Weary"

In a Savior's love abiding,
There is found a blissful rest;
For the Lord is then providing,
And fulfills the soul's request.

Chorus

There is sweet rest in Jesus;
There is sweet rest in Jesus;
There is sweet rest in Jesus,
There is rest for you.
On this side death's rolling Jordan,
In a present, full salvation,
Where "tis heaven below" to love him.
There is rest for you.

Inbred sin is fully vanquished,
Jesus bids it all depart,
With his fullness fills the spirit,
Reigns triumphant in the heart.

Chorus

Love and boldness, faith and patience,
In this lovely fragrant clime,
Neath the Spirit's gracious showers,
Bloom in beauty all the time.

Chorus

Death itself has lost its terrors,
Satan too is overcome.
Shout for gladness, saints of Jesus,
As you journey toward your home.

9

Canaan: Spiritual Sunshine (Continued)

Prelude

FOR THE LORD THY God bringeth thee into a good land, a land of brooks of water, of fountains and depths that spring out of valleys and hills; a land of wheat, and barley, and vines, and fig trees, and pomegranates; a land of olive oil and honey; a land wherein thou shalt eat bread without scarceness, thou shalt not lack any thing in it; a land whose stones are iron, and out of whose hills thou mayest dig brass. When thou hast eaten and art full, then thou shalt bless the Lord thy God for the good land he hath given thee. — Deut. 8:7, 10.

Blessed are they who do hunger and thirst after righteousness; for they shall be filled.— Matt. 5: 6.

And God is able to make all grace abound towards you; that ye, always having all sufficiency in all things, may abound to every good work. —2 Cor. 9:8.

> A land of corn, and wine, and oil,
> Favored with God's peculiar smile,
> With every blessing blest;
> There dwells the Lord our righteousness,
> And keeps his own in perfect peace
> And everlasting rest.

Canaan: Spiritual Sunshine (Continued)

IN CANAAN THE TONGUES of the people were to be controlled by love. "Thou shalt not go up and down as a talebearer among thy people." (Lev. 19:16.) In spiritual Egypt and the "Crooked-path Wilderness" the tongue runs wild, and "no man can tame it." In a justified state the great Tongue-Tamer has captured and bound it, and in spiritual Canaan, by the power of love divine, he has tamed it and now uses it mightily for his glory. Thrice happy are all who surrender their tongues to the absolute control of Jesus Christ. Nevermore shall such shoot

"poisoned arrows" of gossip and slander, or speak "filthy communi-
cations," or "foolish jesting," or "idle" or "hasty" words, to the grief
of loved ones and the glee of Satan; but their King shall "keep them
secretly in a pavilion from the strife of tongues," and of his righteousness "shall they talk all the day long;" "For they cannot but
speak the things which they have seen and heard."

In Canaan the people were to render a joyous service. Otherwise all of the
numberless and rich blessings of the promised land would be forfeited, and all
the awful curse pronounced by God should be experienced. "Because thou
servest not the Lord thy God *with joyfulness* and *with gladness of heart*, for
the abundance of all things; therefore shalt thou serve thine enemies ... in
hunger, and in thirst, and in want of all things; and he shall put a yoke of iron
upon thy neck, until be have destroyed thee. Moreover all of these curses shall
come upon thee, and shall pursue thee, and overtake thee, till thou be destroyed." (Deut. 28:47, 48, 45.)

The parallel Canaan experience of the believer echoes the same thought. If
he loses the "joy of the Lord," like Samson he loses his "strength," and soon
becomes a prey to the enemy. There may be "heaviness through manifold
temptations," but beneath it all there will be a joyous response to all the King's
behests. In spiritual Egypt and in the wilderness experience of the backslider
there is "no service" for Christ; in a justified state there is "poor" and "slow"
service; but in spiritual Canaan there is joyous service.

It is said that an employer paying his workmen gave one of them
double wages. "Wherefore this?" exclaimed the surprised laborer. "I have
done no more than others."

"I do not pay you for doing more work," was the response, "but for the *way
you have done it*. You have gone about your work with a light step, a sunny
smile, and a merry song, and worked *in such a way* that it is worth double pay
to have you around." May we each ever serve God in such a manner that it
will "be worth double pay" to him to "have us around!"

All that God promised to Israel in Canaan was verified. "There failed
not aught of any good thing which the Lord had spoken to Israel; all
came to pass." (Josh, 21:45.) In spiritual Canaan the believer in a similar
way proves the faithfulness of the divine promises. "All his needs" are
supplied. "All grace abounds towards him; so that, having all-sufficiency
in all things, he abounds in every good work." He realizes that "He is

faithful who hath promised," and that "though the heavens and earth should pass away," yet his word "abideth forever." His heartsong is:

> *Jesus, Jesus, how I trust him,*
> *How I've proved him o'er and o'er!*
> *Jesus, Jesus, blessed Jesus!*
> *O for grace to trust him more!*

Such would as quickly steal as to question the veracity of their "covenant-keeping" King.

In Canaan their conquest of the territory assigned them was gradual. "And the Lord shall put out those nations before ye little by little." (Deut. 7:22.) The dwellers in spiritual Canaan are to conquer this world for Christ in a similar way. Like the "leaven" in the meal, the truths they exemplify in their lives shall spread "until all is leavened." One by one individuals came to Jesus at first; then, under the Spirit's power, they were conquered by hundreds and thousands; and now "nations at their base are crumbling," and one after another the kingdoms of this world are becoming those of our Lord and of his Christ.

> *From victory unto victory*
> *His armies he shall lead,*
> *Till every foe is vanquished,*
> *And Christ is Lord indeed.*

All glory to his name!

The children of Israel were commanded to publicly profess that they had come into Canaan.

> And it shall he that when thou art come in unto the land which the Lord thy God giveth thee for an inheritance, and possessest it, and dwellest therein; that thou shalt take of the first of all the fruit of the earth, which thou shalt bring of thy land that the Lord thy God giveth thee, and shalt put it in a basket, and shalt go unto the place which the Lord thy God shall choose to place his name there. And thou shalt go to the priest that shall be in those days, and say unto him, *I profess this day unto the Lord thy God, that I am come unto the country which the Lord sware unto our fathers for to give us* ... The Lord brought us forth out of Egypt with a mighty hand. And he hath brought us into this place, and hath given us this land, even a land that floweth with milk and honey. (Deut. 26:1-3, 8, 9.)

As they were to publicly profess the reception of these spiritual blessings, so are we to thus profess the reception of the greater spiritual blessings of which theirs were the types. As their profession was to be immediately on entering the land, so is ours. Theirs was to be accompanied by the "first-fruits" of the land; ours is to be accompanied with the first-fruits of the Spirit, which are complete submission to God, and complete trust, in the present time, for full salvation. Their profession without the fruit would have been unacceptable; so would ours. Their profession was based upon God's declaration that the land they were in was the one that he had promised them; ours, when we fully submit and trust, rests upon a like eternal foundation. Theirs was in public, in the "place" of worship "unto the priest;" ours, too, must be "before men." As they were to profess both by "fruit" and "words," so are we both by our "life" and our "lips."

They professed a twofold blessing: 1. Deliverance "out of Egypt;" and 2. "Into a land that floweth with milk and honey." We should do likewise: 1. Deliverance from the guilt, penalty, power, and love of sin; and 2. Into purity, power, perfect love, and the fullness of the Spirit.

In their profession they were humble, and gave God the glory. The "I am come unto the country" of verse 3, is quickly followed by the statement that *God gave it*; and in verses 8, 9, that it was *he* that "brought us forth out of Egypt" and "into this place." Dwellers in spiritual Canaan feel the same way. That they are monuments of a mighty deliverance they know, and dare not deny, and also that all the glory is due to their Savior they will never cease to declare.

The devil sometimes whispers to people when they come to this point: "Such a profession will savor of spiritual pride." What ridiculous nonsense! Just as much would it savor of pride for a poor fellow who was helplessly sinking in the quicksand to tell of his deliverance, and praise the man who rescued him.

Some teachers, who ought to know better, duped by the enemy in this respect, are saying, "Profess by your life alone; don't tell it." Had they lived in Canaan, they would have said to the people, as they went to the temple to obey God in this particular, "Take your fruit as God told you, but disobey him in regard to professing with your lips; keep your mouth shut."

Such sometimes admit that people ought to profess deliverance from spiritual Egypt; but when they come to talking about Canaan, they at once feel like protesting, and sometimes say, as one did to Brother William Taylor when he first professed the fullness: "Sit down." Such ought to remember that their advice cannot be followed without disobeying God and grieving the Spirit; and that many of the operations of the Spirit within, such as his witness with ours, union of the soul with God, and the peace that passeth understanding, can be made known to others only by oral testimony. The believer who will not tell what God has done for him is like a man rescued from drowning by another at the peril of his life, and who, notwithstanding this, pretends that he swam ashore. Honesty demands that, simply, humbly, and gladly, we *tell* as well as we can what the Lord hath done for us. In spiritual Canaan the people love to do this.

In Canaan the children of Israel were a compact Church organization. "The Lord hath chosen Zion." (Psa. 132:13.) What Zion was to them the "Church of the firstborn" is in spiritual Canaan. Any movement or experience that is opposed to Scriptural Church organization and discipline is born not of holiness, but of fanaticism.

Last winter at Lyons the main body of the Grand River was completely blocked up by ice. The result was that the river burst its banks, and cutting a new channel, in triumph rolled on upon its mission. The Church has been blocked up in a similar way at different periods by formality, worldliness, and traditions. But this "river" that "makes glad the city of our God," like the Grand, has burst her banks and majestically rolled onward. One outbreak occurred at Pentecost, another in Luther's day, another in Wesley's, and the next will come when men are foolish enough to try again the ice blockade just mentioned; but the "river" will roll onward until lost amid the streets of the eternal city.

Reuben and Gad, because of their "cattle," chose their portion on the east side of Jordan, settled down there, and were the first to be carried away by the enemy. Their action and its results illustrate the peril of settling down in an experience short of the spiritual Canaan which God promises. Beware of resting, because of "cattle," or "horses," or "more land," or aught else, until "filled with the Spirit."

In Canaan God himself was their guide, their defense, and their salvation. "Hear, O Israel, ye approach this day unto battle against your enemies: let not your hearts faint; fear not, and do not tremble, neither be ye terrified because of them; for the Lord your God is he that goeth with you to fight for you against your enemies to save you." (Deut.20:3, 4.) He is all of this to those who are fully his in their conflicts with spiritual foes. "He directs their paths," "gives them power over all the power of the enemy," "saves them out of all their troubles," gives them "good success," grants them his "joy" and "peace" and "glory," "manifests himself" unto them, dwells "within their hearts," gives them the "Holy Spirit," makes them "more than conquerors," and is "with them always, even unto the end." Doubtless through him they are to be the "invincibles" of the universe.

In Canaan the people enjoyed "head," "heart," "hand," "home," and "heaven" religion.

> Therefore shall ye lay up these my words into your "heart" and in your soul, and bind them for a sign upon your "hand," that they may be as frontlets between your eyes. And ye shall teach them your children, speaking of them when thou sittest in thine "house," and when thou walkest by the way, when thou liest down, and when thou risest up. And thou shalt write them upon the doorposts of thine "house," and upon thy gates: that your days may be multiplied, and the days of your children, in the land which the Lord sware unto your fathers to give them, *as the days of heaven upon earth.* (Deut. 11:18-21.)

The above is a Scriptural photograph of the individual and home life of the faithful, as God planned it to be in the earthly Canaan. In spiritual Canaan it becomes a blissful realization.

1. *Head religion.* God's words can reach the heart only through the head, and one reason why some people have so few of God's words in their hearts is because they have been too busy, or lazy, or negligent to store them in their heads.

2. *Heart religion.* In spiritual Canaan the "heart is right," and it is kept with "all diligence." The "word of Christ dwells in it richly," and the King himself is crowned therein. It is pure and full of love. Forgiveness and all the graces of the Spirit make it their headquarters. The law of God is indelibly graven on its walls, and the Gospel atmosphere, fresh from heaven, fills every apartment. A person without heart religion is like a house in the frigid zone without any fire. Without "head" religion he is like the same house without any chimney. The two must not be sundered.

3. *Hand religion.* The dwellers of spiritual Canaan, having "washed them in innocency," "lift up holy hands without wrath or doubting," and "whatsoever their hands find to do," that do they with their might. They

gladly extend their hands in forgiveness, friendship, and benevolence, and expect to employ them in high and holy service for evermore.

4. *Home religion.* In spiritual Canaan the home is a miniature Church; and as people are always good at Church, and as their Church never is out, they are always good. There is no fretting, complaining, or faultfinding. The home is warmed by the heat of holy love, lighted with more than electric radiance by divine truth, supplied abundantly with bread from above and water from the great fountain of living waters, and each member is clad with a wedding suit of righteousness presented by the King.

There is no friction; for all of the spiritual machinery of the household is lubricated by the "oil of gladness," which is freely given to all the faithful. Their spiritual diseases have all been healed, and remedies provided to prevent a relapse. As "they that wait upon the Lord renew their strength," and they are always waiting on him, their strength is ever increasing. As no good thing is withheld from them that walk uprightly, and they are always walking uprightly, their lives are replete with good things. As they believe in "singing with the spirit and understanding also," they have melody such as angels love to hear. Rejoicing evermore with joy unspeakable and full of glory, they have holy ecstasies that speech is utterly powerless to express. Loving God with all the heart, it is their highest joy to live in such a way as to please him.

Loving each other as themselves, they feel as the little girl did when asked to define happiness. She said, "It is to feel as if you wanted to give up all your things to your little sister." It is true that it is needful sometimes to rebuke, but that is done in love, and each soon learn. to feel: "Let the righteous smite me, it shall be a kindness; and let him reprove me, it shall be an excellent oil which shall not break my head." They believe in witnessing for Jesus, and you cannot make them believe that public service is the only place to do it. They mention the story of their wonderful salvation at home, and repeat it daily with a thousand variations, teaching it and all that the Lord commands to their children; making mention of these things when "sitting" and "walking" and "lying down," illustrating gospel truths upon the walls of their houses by fitting pictures and mottoes, and also instructing by papers, books, and songs. The parents gather their children about them at the family altar, and each joins in that sacred and joyous service.

At the table, with heartfelt gratitude, the gracious Father is remembered, and they have gladly promised not to eat, drink, say or do any thing that they cannot ask him to bless them in. What a contrast to homes that devour God's blessing like pigs in their pens, without one expression of thanksgiving to the Giver! What a contrast to the godless homes of some professors, where tobacco using, or cards, or dancing, or novel reading, or perhaps all of these combined, are substituted instead of the proper externals of "home religion!"

4. *Heaven religion.*[1] "A 'home' is known by its fruits." "That your days may be multiplied, and the days of your children, *as the days of heaven on earth.*" In the Canaan experience God's will is "done on earth as it is in heaven." Heaven is cheerful submission to God's will. Hence spiritual Canaan is heaven on earth. With its possessors heaven already is gained, and whether they do service in "heaven below" or "heaven above" is one to them. They wisely leave that to heaven's King. They do not talk about "weathering the blasts of this unfriendly world, and finally gaining heaven," for they have "gained heaven" already. They do not talk about their "trials and tribulations," because these are all sanctified to their good, and they find heavenly bliss in bearing them.

They do not make wry, sour faces when persecuted, but "rejoice and are exceeding glad." Instead of whining about temptations when they come, they resist them, and "count it all joy." Instead of feeling slighted or hurt by any neglects that they may chance to experience, they are so conscious of the presence and favor of the Almighty Maker and Ruler of all universes that a thousand little worlds like this might turn them the "cold shoulder," and it would not destroy their enjoyment. Death to them is changed from the cruel, greedy monster that he once seemed to a kind messenger, employed by their Father to hand them their "promotion papers." They find Jesus more than a match for even "weak nerves."

Many have had an experience similar to that of Rev. F. M. Griffith, who wrote:

Of late some lifelong opinions of mine have been swept away.

1. I thought Beulah songs, light, glory, were for the dying only; yet to poor, weak, sinful me they were given for days, weeks, months, and still I lived. In the unutterable rapture I kept on thinking, "I shall certainly go over the river *soon*, perhaps today." This lesson I have learned. Beulah is at our doors. All believers, even though in perfect health, may enter in.

2. I thought that spiritual rapture need not be looked for in the pressure of certain diseases. I argued, "It can hardly co-exist with a disorder that blunts, overslaughs, and paralyzes the whole nervous system." So in the dropsy that

overflowed me, when swollen to enormous proportions, with no more nervous feeling than a post, I kept on saying, "I am safe; my feet are on the rock; but feeling, emotion, is not now possible. I rest content!" But, brethren, the unspeakable joy, the supernatural glory swept down on me during the prevalence of dropsy (my last attack), and my theory gasped and died.

The lesson taught me is *this*: Spiritual life, joy, rapture, are not necessarily dependent upon, or connected with, physical or nervous conditions. Let the whole nervous system be paralyzed and dead, the spiritual body we have, which is indeed our true life, may thrill with untold ecstasy.

Praise God that such triumphs may be ours even here! Thus "head," "heart," "hand," and "heaven" religion become a blessed reality to all in spiritual Canaan. How gracious in our Father to grant such privileges! Had he given us a "bread and water" experience, and held us at arm's length for a few thousand years, and then permitted this blessedness to dawn on us "little by little," we would have felt even then highly favored; but instead of that, he redeems us from Egypt's dungeons, "breaks every chain," bears our souls to some "glory" summit, and then, when we gasp with unutterable astonishment and joy, and say, "This indeed is heaven and good enough for me forever," he points beyond and above to limitless vistas of increasingly glorious unfoldings, and whispers: "My child, if faithful, your future is ever to be from glory unto glory."

Blessed Beulah land of light, of purity, of power, of liberty, of love, and joyful service, thou art indeed a heaven on earth and the antechamber to the Father's many mansioned house above! Thy fruits are inexpressibly sweet, and thy waters of untold purity. Thy companionships are all rulers, with fadeless crowns and crumbleless kingdoms!

Led by our Father's hand, we have entered thy borders, to remain until our eyes, accustomed to thy glory, which dazzles us so at first, shall be able to bear the brighter revelations beyond; and then, although we shall be ascending forever and forever, we never shall forget that thou wert the place where first we were honored by the abiding presence of the "King in his beauty," and felt the weighty raptures of his perfect love. Earthly expressions are powerless to fittingly magnify thy excellences. In the courts above, when our powers of thought and expression shall have increased a million-fold, and we can call to our assistance the multitudes of the redeemed and the mighty hosts of angels, then shall we be better able to express our value of thy worth!

Endnote

1. For a fuller development of this thought, see *Christ Crowned Within*, chap. 17.

10

Out of Canaan into Babylon

Prelude

YET THEY TEMPTED AND provoked the most high God, and kept not his testimonies: but turned back, and dealt unfaithfully like their fathers; they were turned aside like a deceitful bow. For they provoked him to anger with their high places, and moved him to jealousy with their graven images. When God heard this he was wroth, and greatly abhorred Israel ... and delivered his strength into captivity and his glory into the enemies' hand. Psa. 78:56-59, 61.

For it had been better for them not to have known the way of righteousness than, after they have known it, to turn from the holy commandment delivered unto them. —2 Peter 2:21.

> *When from God our hearts decline,*
> *How we fall from heights sublime!*
> *When his warnings we despise,*
> *What a sight for angel eyes!*
> *When his judgments we'll not heed,*
> *How at last our hearts must bleed!*
> *Warned by Israel's awful state,*
> *May we wisely shun her fate!*

Out of Canaan into Babylon

"IF YE BE WILLING and obedient, ye shall eat the good of the land; but if ye refuse and rebel, ye shall be devoured with the sword: for the mouth of the Lord hath spoken it." (Psa. 1:19, 20.)

"And Nebuchadnezzar, king of Babylon, came against the city, and his servants did besiege it ... And he carried away all Jerusalem, and all the princes, and all the mighty men of valor, even ten thousand captives and all the craftsmen and smiths; none remained, save the poorest sort of the people of the land." (2 Kings 24:11,14.)

How differently history often runs from what we wish! How much grander if the children of Israel had kept their covenant, and triumphantly retained Canaan, instead of falling from it! As it is, this portion of their history presents a vivid picture of kindred occurrences which transpire with believers, who, proving unfaithful, fall from spiritual Canaan, into the oppressive Babylon of awful condemnation. It was one thing for Israel to enter Canaan, and another quite as great to remain there. The same is true of all who enter spiritual Canaan. To be forewarned is to be forearmed. Instructed by their awful example, foolish indeed will we be if we follow in their downward steps.

"Princes," "mighty men," "men of valor," "chief singers," and "priests" were carried into "captivity." Similar features can be traced in the spiritual photograph. Neither governmental and ecclesiastical positions, nor educational and religious advantages, nor long residence in the land of perfect love, will deliver from spiritual captivity, when the divinely decreed conditions of possession are ruthlessly cast aside.

"And Israel served the Lord all the days of Joshua, and all the days of the elders that overlived Joshua, and which had known all the works of the Lord that he had done for Israel." (Josh. 24:31.) Thus we see that they "retained the goodly land" for a long time; and if they were able to retain it that long, surely they, by God's grace, might have ever kept it if they would. The deeds whereby they forfeited it are photographs of those whereby believers forfeit their Canaan of perfect love.

They became covenant-breakers. "The children of Israel have forsaken thy covenant, thrown down thine altars, and slain thy prophets with the sword." (1 Kings 19:16.) "They are turned back to the iniquities of their forefathers which refused to hear my words, and they went after other gods to serve them. The house of Israel and the house of Judah have broken my covenant which I made with their fathers." (Jer. 11:10.)

Thus the solemn covenant which they had made with God was broken. They had promised to *"do all"* and *"go anywhere,"* that God might direct. This pledge they persistently broke; and thus forfeited their inheritance. Spiritual Canaan is lost in a like way. A broken covenant is a swift and sure chariot to perdition.

They would not listen to the truth. "Refused to hear my words." Their brethren in spiritual realms do likewise. Having sinned against it, they "will not come to the light lest their deeds should be reproved." They don't like spiritual papers, people, or preachers. They may be willing to talk theories; but to listen to commands, promises, or experiences that teach deep spirituality is *against their will*. They thus place themselves among the number of whom it is written: "He that turneth away his ear from hearing the law, even his prayer shall be abomination."

They neglected worship. "Thrown down thine altars." Like their parents in the garden, they sinned against God, and then were afraid to meet him. Covenant breaking in spiritual Canaan unrepented of is followed by like results. Private, family, and public devotions, "Scripture searching" and "fasting," are either forsaken or become a mere form.

"They went after other gods to serve them." Ashteroth, Baal, and Moloch drew them to their shrines, and their idolatry, in God's sight, was treason. In spiritual Canaan similar treachery produces similar results. What Ashteroth, "Queen of heaven, sitting on a lion, her head surrounded by the sun's rays, and in one hand a thunderbolt and the other a scepter" —was to them, a "popular religion" becomes to spiritual believers. They cease complete trust in God, and adopt a sort of "lion," "sunshine," and "thunderbolt and scepter" religion. They seek a religion that will be outwardly popular, pompous, and dazzling, and at the same time "fleshly" and easy.

Their *hearts* worship at such a shrine as this, and as they bow there the "crowns" fall from their heads. All heaven echoes "treason!" and God thunders: "Cursed be the man that trusteth in man, and maketh flesh his arm, and whose heart departeth from the Lord; for he shall be like the heath in the desert, and shall not see when good cometh; but shall inhabit the parched places in the wilderness, in a salt land and not inhabited."

They "sacrificed their children" by fire to Moloch. What Moloch was to them the "god of this world is to believers." We lift our hands in horror as we think of parents placing their sons and daughters upon Moloch's heated pyres, until they are consumed before their eyes; but fathers and mothers who, by either precept or example, teach their children to "gain wealth" for wealth's sake instead of Christ's; to "gain knowledge and position" for the "applause of men" instead of the plaudits of the Eternal; to marry for position in society instead of heaven's holy motive; to care more for man's opinion than God's — are offering them upon an altar as cruel as Moloch's; an altar, the pyre of which is heated by the fire of hell, where, unless a miracle interpose, its victims must make their eternal home.

Upon the brows of such parents, who once were high in heavenly favor, the angel prints the awful words, "Thy glory is departed;" and, louder than the applause of giddy worldlings or the plaudits from the pit beneath, rolls to their startled souls the voice of God Almighty, saying: "Their blood will I require at thine hand."

The systems of idolatry to which falling Israel conformed were simply agencies for the gratification of the carnal nature through the *lusts of the flesh* and the *love of the world*. With the believer in Beulah Land, any yielding to the world, flesh, or devil has in it the seed of idolatry, and if cherished will drive from the land. These enemies remain to seek his ruin, and must be conquered, not loved nor served.

Chiefly instrumental in Israel's downfall was their compromising matters with the idolatrous inhabitants of the land. Instead of "driving them out" of the land and "destroying them," as they were commanded, they "took tribute" of them, "made leagues," and finally "intermarried" with them. The most heinous of their after sins can be traced to this compromising spirit. Their idolatrous confederates thus became "thorns in their sides," which finally pierced through to their very heart. Compromises as to "companionships," "society," "profession," "soul-saving work," "property," "business," and perhaps "little matters," have often in the end cost spiritual Canaan. To yield any is to invite ruin.

Israel's downfall began with "negligence" and "forgetfulness." Believers need trumpet-tongued warnings of the same dangers. While men "sleep" the slumber of "negligence" and "forgetfulness," the enemy into the heart fountain pours poisoned waters of depravity that at once flow forth into a woeful stream.

Israel engaged in profitless undertakings. "My people have changed their glory for that which did not profit." (Jer. 2:11.) Holiness people who engage in profitless thoughts, words, or deeds, do so at like peril.

Israel sank through willful ignorance. "Therefore my people are gone into captivity, because they have no knowledge." (Isa. 5:13.) All needful knowledge through God was accessible to them, but her leaders willfully rejected it, and the masses, all too willingly, followed in their footsteps. Thousands, "alienated from the life of God through the ignorance that is in them," have perished in a similar way. Breaking their covenant with God, they lose experimental knowledge of spiritual things, and thus become an easy prey to the enemy. Others begin right; but, refusing to prayerfully study the Word and read holy books and papers that wo ld help to guide them aright, they ignorantly stumble into the black ditch of fanaticism, and sink beneath its slime.

Israel disregarded correction. "For the people turneth not unto him that smiteth them, neither do they seek the Lord of hosts." (Isa. 9:13.) When believers begin to decline, God speaks, and then often chastises. If penitent, they kiss with gratitude the hand that brings the chastisement; but if; like Israel, they "turn not unto him," they thus reveal a sad perversity of soul.

The leaders of the people did much to hasten Israel's downfall. "For the leaders of this people cause them to err; and they that are led of them are destroyed." (Jer. 9:16.) Many have fallen from spiritual Canaan by looking to "leaders" instead of to Jesus. Follow others only as "they follow Christ." "Fix your eyes upon Jesus."

Babylonish captivity was also invited by the treachery of false ministers. Its counterpart in the spiritual world in a like manner receives many victims through the same agency. As they had so important a part in Israel's ruin, and their generation still lives to carry on their "wolfish" work, we will stop and view their Scriptural photograph. God hangs it up in the gallery of his Word, for the protection of his people in all ages, just as the government sometimes, for the protection of its citizens, posts descriptions of desperados in public places through all its realms. All the features mentioned may not be found in any one of them, but often enough combine to establish their detection. I suppose Jesus referred to these features when he said, "By their fruits ye shall know them."

(a) *They went without being sent.* They chose preaching, as men choose ordinary occupations, with no call from God. They spurned the divine declaration that "no man taketh this honor to himself, but him that is called, as was Aaron;" and God said of them: "I have not sent these prophets, yet they ran: I have not spoken unto them, yet they prophesied." (Jer. 23:21.)

(b) *They were light and treacherous.* "Her prophets are light and treacherous persons; her priests have polluted the sanctuary; they have done violence to the law." (Zech. 3:4.) They were light and trifling, instead of "serious, weighty, solemn;" "treacherous," in that their whole deportment thus belied the messages given to their cure. Their brethren of to-day have been known to "crack jokes," and tell "light" and sometimes "low" stories for hours; to join in the amusements of giddy world-lings, and in thousands of ways give expression to a levity that is born of the pit.

(c) *They were sacrilegious.* They "polluted the sanctuary." Jesus caught them at it when below, and the snapping of his "scourge of cords," as he drove them from his temple, has annoyed their fraternity ever since. His command, "Make not my Father's house an house of merchandise," they have never been slow to break. Their brethren today do not hesitate to sanction worldly entertainments and traffic in sanctuaries that have been dedicated to the worship of God only. If Jesus with holy indignation drove the "buyers and sellers," with all their wares, from the outer court of an earthly temple, what would he do with those who desecrate the very place that should be sacred as the birthplace of souls?

(d) *"They did violence" to the law.* This was done in three ways,—by breaking it, by neglecting to preach it, and by preaching only a part of it. Today they treat the gospel, which includes the moral law, in a similar way.

(e) *They cared more for the fleece than the flock.* "The priests thereof teach for hire, and the prophets thereof divine for money; yet will they lean upon the Lord, and say, Is not the Lord among as? none evil can come upon us. Therefore for your sake shall Zion be plowed as a field, and Jerusalem shall become heaps, and the mountain of the house as the high places of the forest." (Micah 3:11, 12.) Such are more anxious about their salaries than the salvation of souls, and appointments where they can get gain than those where they can do good. They speed souls Babylonward, and the ruin they have wrought is appalling.

(f) *They prophesied smooth things, crying, Peace, peace, when there was no peace.* "They have healed the hurt of the daughter of my people slightly, saying, Peace, peace, when there is no peace." (Jer. 6:14.) One of them, by accident I suppose, once said something in a sermon that so convicted a sinner that he wept. The preacher at once apologized with, "I did not mean to hurt your feelings." They will tell people that they are converted or sanctified before God does. They offer "peace" on condi-tions that God does not endorse, and that will not stand the test of the dying hour and judgment.

(g) *They preached falsehoods.* "The prophets prophesy falsely, and the priests bear rule by their means; and my people love to have it so: and what will ye do in the end thereof?" (Jer. 5:31.) Their brethren today do not scruple to do likewise, and there are not wanting those who "love to have it so." But what of the end?

(h) *They would not walk in the holiness highway.* "Thus saith the Lord, Stand ye in the ways and see, and ask for the old paths, where is the good way, and walk therein, and ye shall find rest for your souls. But they said, We will not walk therein." (Jer. 6:16.)

(i) *They stole their sermons.* "Therefore behold, I am against the prophets, saith the Lord, that steal my words every one from his neighbor." (Jer. 23:30.) Their brethren of the present day are accused of following in their footsteps.

(j) *They neglected pastoral visitation.* "Therefore thus saith the Lord God of Israel against the pastors that feed my people, Ye have scattered my flock, and driven them away, and *have not visited them.* Behold I will visit upon you the evil of your doings, saith the Lord." (Jer. 23:2.) False preachers; pastoral visitation distasteful and neglected; flock scattered; preacher visited by God for the evil,—who covets such a record?

(k) *They were "dressy," popularity-seeking, grasping, and itched for office.* "Then in the audience of all the people he said unto his disciples, Beware of the scribes, which desire to walk in long robes, and love greetings in the markets, and the highest seats in the synagogues, and the chief rooms at feasts; which devour widows' houses, and for a pretense make long prayers; the same shall receive greater damnation." (Luke 20:45-47.)

(l) *They fretted for honorary titles.* "And greetings in the markets, and to be called of men, Rabbi, Rabbi." (Matt. 23:7.) Who would be willing to expose his ignorance by maintaining that this unfortunate generation has passed away?

(m) *They made social calls with selfish motives.* "Thus saith the Lord God unto the shepherds, Woe to the shepherds of Israel that do feed themselves! Should not the shepherds feed the flocks? Ye eat the fat, and ye clothe you with the wool, ye kill them that are fed; but ye feed not the flock." (Ezekiel 34:2, 3.) They visited to fill their stomachs, not to feed the flock. It is to be hoped that their generation is extinct.

(n) *They were arbitrary and exacting in their administration.* "The diseased have ye not strengthened, neither have ye healed that which was sick, neither have ye bound up that which was broken, neither have ye brought again that which was driven away, neither have ye sought again that which was lost; but with force and with *cruelty* have ye ruled them." (Ezek. 34:4.)

(o) *They were wrong on the temperance question.* "The priest and the prophet have erred through strong drink: they are out of the way through strong drink; they err in vision, they stumble in judgment: for all tables are full of vomit and filthiness, so that there is no place clean." (Isa. 28:7, 8.) Evidently this class believed in either free liquor or license, drank when they pleased; and the last verse quoted almost compels to the conclusion that the generally received history of tobacco is wrong, and that they were also slaves to the spittoon. This age is cursed by their counterpart.

(p) *They preached their own "views" instead of God's Word.* "They speak a vision of their own heart, and not out of the mouth of the Lord." (Jer.23:16.) They did not live near enough to God to hear his voice, and so out of their own heart they spun the spider-web speeches which they substituted for messages divine. What a farce! And yet who has not seen it repeated?

(q) *They encouraged people in unscriptural ideas and practices.* "They say unto every one that walketh after the imagination of his own heart, No evil shall come upon you." (Isa. 23:17. Such may get the goodwill of those whom thus they deceive for a little time, but it will be to burn under their reproaches through eternity!

(r) *They were strangers to converting and sanctifying grace.* "The priests said not, Where is the Lord? And they that handle the law *knew me not.*" (Jer.2:8.) "Blind leaders of the blind," what wonder that "they both fall into the ditch?" The devil's "ditches," in all ages, have been kept full by such "handlers of the law."

(s) *They were immoral.* "For both prophet and priest are profane." (Isa. 22:11.) "They commit adultery and walk in lies; they strengthen the hands also of evil doers." (Isa. 22:14.) They are seldom openly so, yet the priestly wickedness of Jeremiah's day and the clerical orgies of the Middle Ages, as well as the occasional exposures of the present day, show that this class of "false prophets" has never been without representatives.

(t) *God calls them "wind" prophets.* (Jer. 5:13.) And such they are—hot winds from the desert, carrying blight and blasting wherever they smite; poisonous winds from the malarious swamps and marshes of sin, bearing spiritual typhoid, that ends in the agonies of death eternal. "Beware of false prophets." (Jesus) "Beloved, believe not every spirit; but try the spirits whether they be of God: for many false prophets are gone out into the world." (1 John 4:1.)

(u) *Their end is to be horrible beyond description.* Having deceived and ruined many on earth, they are next represented as attempting to deceive the Almighty on his judgment throne, saying: "Lord, Lord, have we not prophesied in thy name? and in thy name cast out devils? and in thy name done many wonderful works?" Then they shall be "cast alive into a lake of fire burning with brimstone," "where the beast and the false prophet are, and shall be tormented day and night for ever and ever."

(v) *False prophets abounded among the Jews at Babylon.* (Jer. 29:16.) A Babylonish condition of the Church is favorable to their development, and hence they seek to conserve it. Attention has thus been called to "false prophets," not in a censorious spirit, but because they were the chief agents contributing to Israel's downfall and captivity, and having exerted a like influence in the Church in all ages, *are still continuing to do so*; and because this warning is a part of the gospel, no portion of which should be put under a bushel.

What a contrast are these "false" prophets to the noble, self-sacrificing prophets and preachers of today and all the ages, who have "declared the whole counsel of God;" "with tears" have sought souls from "house to house;" have braved the raging elements of the material world and the world of darkness to save men, and, "laying down their lives for the sheep," have triumphantly ascended to their heavenly mansions, leaving examples that have inspired thousands to follow them as they followed Christ!

By the sins mentioned, and many more that might be, Israel fell, until she was so low that Isaiah said, "O sinful nation, a people laden with iniquity, a seed of evil-doers, children that are corrupters; they have forsaken the Lord, they have provoked the Holy One of Israel to anger, they have gone away backward." (Isa. 1:4.) As a result of their sinfulness, *"in those days the Lord began to cut Israel short."* (2 Kings 10:32.) What it means to be "cut short," every backslider from spiritual Canaan knows by bitter experience. *Many of them retained the form of worship without the power.* Such are spiritual corpses.

Their formal worship was unacceptable and offensive to God. "I hate, I despise your feast days, and I will not smell in your solemn assemblies. Though ye offer me burnt offerings and your meat offerings, I will not accept them; neither will I regard the peace offerings of your fat beasts. Take thou away from me the noise of thy songs; for I will not hear the melody of thy viols. But let judgment run down as waters, and righteousness as a mighty stream." (Amos 5:21-24.)

What was true of Israel as she was thus nearing Babylon, is true of all who renounce the "mind of Christ." Though they may continue their worship, "speak and sing with the tongues of men and angels," gave all their goods to feed the poor," and their bodies to be burned," yet, in God's sight, their mock worship is an offense which he "despises," and which he commands to "be taken away." Well may formal Babylonish worshippers tremble; for God is angry, and his judgments will not tarry long.

Israel, by falling from Canaan, caused others to stumble. "Because my people have forgotten me, they have burned incense to vanity, and they have caused them to stumble in their ways from the ancient paths, to walk in paths in a way not cast up." (Jer. 18:15.) Probably no one ever fell from spiritual Canaan to spiritual Babylon without causing others to stumble with him. What a mighty incentive to steadfastness!

Israel, in falling, became guilty of soul-murder. "Also in thy skirts is found *the blood of the souls of the poor innocents.* I have not found it by secret search, but upon all of these." In the parallel spiritual state, people are guilty in a similar way. Children perish because of the unfaithfulness of parents, and doubtless millions of soul-murderers will stand by the side of Cain and Judas in the day of awful reckoning.

The children of Israel were repeatedly warned of their danger. "And the Lord hath sent unto you all his servants the prophets, rising early and sending them; but ye have not hearkened nor inclined your ear to hear." (Jer. 25:4.) Through these faithful messengers God placed before them inexpressibly rich blessing if obedient, and many and awful judgments if faithless. (See Lev. 26, and Deut. 27 and 28.) All who are forfeiting spiritual Canaan are warned in a like manner. The Spirit, the Word, and the Church, in thunder tones, repeatedly voice the warning.

Israel was further warned by preliminary judgments. Seven times was she made captive by the surrounding nations before her final enslavement in faraway Babylon. Gentle warnings, sterner ones; ordinary judgments, severe ones; *final captivity*, — such was the order of God's dealings with them, and is with all who wander from him. O Israel! why wouldst thou not be warned?

Though long delayed and foretold, yet final captivity came to Israel suddenly. "Yea, it shall be *at an instant suddenly.* Thou shalt be visited of the Lord of hosts with thunder, and with earthquake, and great noise, with storm and tempest, and the flame of devouring fire." (Isa. 29:5, 6.) This is God's description of the judgment whereby they were carried into final captivity to Babylon.

It is a graphic picture, also, of his dealings with those who, breaking their covenant, have forfeited spiritual Canaan. O, fallen one! Thou dost hear the spiritual "thunder," "great noise," "storm and tempest;" and feel the spiritual "flame of devouring fire," and quakings of a mighty soul-earthquake. Then art thou in spiritual Babylon, and though long threatening, yet suddenly the dreaded judgment fell. Thy Maker would have had thee singing songs of triumph, instead of uttering those awful wails.

Babylonish captivity was the more bitter to Israel because self incurred. "Thy ways and thy doings have procured these things unto thee." "For ye have kindled a fire in mine anger, which shall burn forever." (Isa. 4:18, and 17:4.) A like consciousness of personal blame possesses those who fall from spiritual Canaan into the awful condemnation of Babylonish bondage. That in itself is a lash that scourges more cruelly than that of any human taskmaster.

Babylonish bondage was worse than "wandering in the wilderness." In the spiritual states illustrated by each, the same is also true.

(a) *Only two tribes returned from Babylon to Canaan, while every tribe emerged from the wilderness.* The more lofty the height that the spirit falls from, the greater is the difficulty of regaining it. Satan was so high and fell so low that he can never get back.

(b) *Babylon was worse than the wilderness because those in the wilderness had never enjoyed the pleasures of Canaan,* and hence were unable to so keenly feel their absence. The spiritual analogy is clear. Those in the "wilderness experience," never having tasted the enjoyments of spiritual Canaan, cannot be pained by their absence as those in spiritual Babylon, who have known all the glories of the land.

(c) *God expressly declares that they were worse than their fathers.* "And ye have done worse than your fathers; for, behold, ye walk every-one after the imagination of his evil heart, that they may not hearken unto me: therefore will I cast you out of this land into a land that ye know not ... where I will not shew you favor." (Jer. 16:12,13.)

They were worse than their fathers in the wilderness: 1. In that they sinned against greater light; 2. Against greater mercies; 3. And their condition was also worse in that God expressly declared that he would "*shew them no favor*," while in the wilderness they were shown many; 4. In the wilderness Moses interceded, and in answer to his prayers Israel as a nation was delivered, while of Israel in Babylon he declared that, "Though Moses and Samuel stood before me, yet my mind could not be towards this people: cast them out of my sight, and let them go forth." (Jer. 15:1.)

The inhabitants of spiritual Babylon, like their brethren then, have sinned against greater light and mercies than those in the spiritual wilderness. Some of them also have doubtless committed the "sin unto death," for which it is useless to pray, and are like the man of whom the Savior said, that the unclean spirit "taketh to himself seven other spirits more wicked than himself, and they enter in and dwell there: and the last state of that man is worse than the first." (Luke 11:26.) In spiritual Egypt the unclean spirit is master of the man; in the Sinai Wilderness (justification) he is bound; in the Desert Wilderness (backsliding) he has broken from bondage, and rules with more than former fury; in spiritual Canaan he is "gone out of the man," and the soul temple is "swept and garnished;" in spiritual Babylon he has returned, and holds carnival with "seven spirits more wicked than himself."

May the horrors of such an experience impel us to shun it as we would hell itself! On the gravestones of all in spiritual Babylon God writes: "O that thou hadst hearkened to my commandments! then had thy peace been as a river, and thy righteousness as the waves of the sea." Who covets such an epitaph?

11

Back From Babylon

Prelude

THUS SAITH THE LORD the God of Israel: Like these good figs, so will I acknowledge them that are carried away captive of Judah, whom I have sent out of this place into the land of the Chaldeans for their good. For I will set mine eyes upon them for good, and I will bring them again unto this land: and I will build them, and not pull them down; and I will plant them, and not pluck them up. And I will give them an heart to know me, that I am the Lord; and they shall be my people, and I will be their God: for they shall return unto me with all their heart.—Jer. 24:5-7.

Turn, O backsliding children, saith the Lord; for I am married unto you: and I will take you one of a city, and two of a family, and I will bring you to Zion.—Jer. 3:14.

> *Though we wander far away,*
> *Christ doth follow day by day.*
> *When affliction's irons we feel,*
> *He is there our wounds to heal.*
> *When from sin our steps we turn,*
> *Then no more his ire will burn,*
> *When we humbly seek his face.*
> *Then he grants all needed grace.*
> *O the depths of love divine!*
> *Soul, this wondrous love is thine.*

Back From Babylon

THE OBJECT OF THIS chapter is to aid and encourage all who may have fallen from spiritual Canaan to at once retrace their steps. May the great Shepherd of the sheep assist in leading each endangered one back into his fold!

God remembered Israel, even in Babylon. By his Word, his Spirit, his prophets, and a few faithful followers, he made his people feel that, though their sins were terrible, yet still he loved them. Though sometimes in sad despair he sighs, "Ephraim is joined to his idols, let him alone," yet soon again he is heard to moan like a mother over the cold form of her only babe: "How shall I give thee up?" Wandering child, as thus thou seest a picture of thy Father's agonizing love and forbearance towards thee, wilt thou not arise and with penitent feet retrace thy sad course, and seek his freely proffered pardon and restoration?

Israel in Babylon had promise of restoration to Canaan. "I will set mine eyes upon them for good, and I will bring them again into this land: and I will build them and not pull them down; and I will plant them and not pluck them up." (Jer. 24:6.) Kindred promises of pardon and favor are extended to the spiritual captive. In this as well as other realms of spiritual bondage, "whosoever will may come," and whosoever "cometh" he will in "no wise cast out." The fact that but comparatively few in Babylon claimed the promise and accepted restoration is an analogy that may alarm; yet the additional fact that all who *would* come were welcomed and delivered, illustrates the fact that not one *yielding penitent* will be left in spiritual Babylon. Glory to God for such a salvation!

Many of the events which transpired at the returning of the captives from Babylon are illustrative of events that take place when those who have fallen from perfect love into spiritual bondage, again return to spiritual Canaan. Wanderers, like them, reach a point where they so feel their bondage and their loss that they cry, *"We are in great distress."* (Neh. 9:37.) If the melodies of the halcyon days gone by flit through the chambers of their souls, lo! they have "hung their harps upon the willow," and feel that they "cannot sing the songs of Zion in a strange land."

Memory sometimes points backward to the seasons when there were "songs in the night," and when "Jerusalem was a joy" and Zion a "praise in the earth;" but quickly then the floodgates of the bitter present are opened, and thoughts of "present captivity," "Jerusalem in ruins," and "Zion demolished," flood the soul with bitterness and woe. Many numberless woes made Israel's cup of "distress" to overflow. The backslider from spiritual Canaan drinks the same cup of "wormwood and of gall."

Those who were rescued from Babylon were the ones who realized their sad condition. Their fellow-captives were fallen perhaps lower, but their fall did not pain them. The same is true with like spiritual captives.

There is much hope for all who sense the bitterness of their captivity, and very little for those who are callous to it.

> *For the bruised reed and the smoking flax,*
> *Weeping may endure for a night,*
> *But joy cometh in the morning!*

The following are some of the steps that the captive took to regain their freedom and long-lost Canaan. Spiritual captives who follow their example will just as surely find the parallel spiritual blessing:

1. *They fasted.* "The children of Israel were assembled with *fasting*, and sackcloth, and earth upon them." (Neh. 9:1.) There is a kind of evil spirit that cometh out "only by prayer and fasting," and it is usually this sort that possesses those who have fallen from high spiritual attainments. When feasting crowds out fasting, the body may grow fat, but the soul will starve to death. Spiritual decline dates back to neglect of fasting, and spiritual exaltation must begin there.

Pentecostal power was attended by Pentecostal fasting. Fasting and self-examination are to the soul what inspection is to the engine, and ignoring in either case means disaster. Let every one in spiritual Babylon say, "I will not eat or drink until I know I am rescued from the pit that in my folly I have digged." Then it will not be long before "distress" and "fasting" are turned into gladness and triumph.

2. *"The children of Israel confessed their sins."* (Neh. 9:3.) They went over the whole catalogue from Egypt until that time, keeping nothing back, toning nothing down. This is another forceful object-lesson for all seeking to regain spiritual Canaan. There should be frank and full confession, without any "ifs," "buts," or "perhaps."

3. *Israel shouldered all the blame*, saying: "Howbeit thou art just in all that is brought upon us; for thou hast done right, but we have done wickedly." (Neh.9:38.) We should feel likewise, for the same is just as true with every wanderer as it was with them; and until we reach a kindred state of mind our Babylonish releasement is hopeless.

4. *"They separated themselves from ungodly associations."* (Neh. 9:2.) As the gold has to be separated from its rough and worthless companion-rocks in the mountain before it can be melted and receive the governmental impress, so must the wanderer draw the line between himself and

giddy worldlings ere he can receive the impress of the government divine. "What concord hath Christ with Belial?"

5. *"They began to study the Word."* (Neh. 9:3.) Like shipwrecked mariners, who, ignoring chart and compass, are nearly wrecked on murderous rocks, and now return to study again the long neglected "guidebook," and take their bearings, so Israel again returns to God's long-neglected Word. Wanderers must do likewise, or with a fearful *crash* be wrecked amid the breakers of eternity.

6. *They renewed their covenant.* They had broken and forsaken it. Now, penitently, they renew their former vows. Under this head they promise again to renounce all companionship with the people of the land, and render to God the "first-fruits of every thing." They soon formed the "consecration covenant" made by their fathers as they entered the land of Jordan; and they "entered into a curse, and into an oath, to walk in God's law, which was given by Moses, the servant of God, and to observe and do all the commandments of the Lord our God, and his judgments and his statutes." (Neh. 10:29.) Heartsick wanderer, wilt thou not just now set again thy seal to these solemn vows that once held thee almost entranced within the realms of spiritual light and life and joy?

7. *They sought God earnestly.* They met the conditions, and claimed this promise which he had given them: "Then shall ye call upon me, and I will hearken unto you. And ye shall seek me and find me, when ye shall search for me *with all your heart.* And I will be found of you, saith the Lord; and I will turn away your captivity." (Jer. 29:12-14.) Kindred promises challenge all who, like them, have wandered. When we, like them, meet the conditions and seek deliverance "with all the heart," then our "captivity" like theirs will be "turned away." For such gracious condescension and mercy on the part of our Father, "let every thing that hath breath praise the Lord!"

8. *The children of Israel began at once the work of reformation.* (a) They returned to Canaan; (b) they rebuilt the temple; (c) they gave for its support, and conducted its worship as God commanded. A consecration that does not find expression in outer acts is false. Good desires, resolutions, and promises would not have brought them back to Canaan if they had not put them in execution. With the seeker of spiritual Canaan the same is true, and *inaction* has cost many a Canaan on earth and heaven hereafter.

Many of the children of Israel at this point had severe struggles in correcting past wrongs. God had positively prohibited their intermarriage with the surrounding nations. This command had been ruthlessly broken, so "that the holy seed 'had' mingled themselves with the people of those lands; yea, the hand of the princes and rulers had been chief in this trespass." (Ezra 9:2.) Ezra "astonied," "ashamed," and "weeping," "cast himself down" before the assembled people, who, with bitter wailings at the thought of their sin and the pain that they had thus brought upon themselves and others, to his exhortation "to make confession unto the Lord God of your fathers and do his pleasure; and separate yourselves from the people of the land and from strange wives," responded, with a loud voice, "As thou hast said so must we do."

"And some of them had wives, by whom they had children." This was one of the "right hands" that must needs be cut off, and the "right eyes" that must needs be plucked out, before God's smile could rest upon them. Nearly all who have wandered far from God have entangled themselves in some similar web. This lesson shows that such strands can and must be broken. The pain it causes cannot be charged to God, but must be to those who disregard his Word. How many at this point have felt—

> *Ye tempting sweets forbear,*
> *Ye dearest idols fall;*
> *My heart, ye cannot share,*
> *For Jesus must have all.*
> *'Tis bitter pain; 'tis cruel smart;*
> *But O, you must consent, my heart!*

It would be infinitely better to lose worlds, and suffer ages, than to cherish the least thing that would shut Jesus from the soul. Agonizing as it may be, no rectification of wrongs in the life that can be remedied should be neglected. To neglect them is but to forge Babylonish chains the tighter, and forever forfeit Canaan.

The children of Israel having met the conditions, trusted God for pardon, protection, and reinstatement in the land which by sin they had forfeited. Let every seeker for re-enthronement in spiritual Canaan wisely and hastily walk in their footsteps. To them God graciously promised, and he repeats it with deep spiritual meaning, to all who thus have wandered: "But if ye turn unto me, and keep my commandments, and do them, though there were of you cast out unto the uttermost part of the heaven, yet will I gather them from thence, and will bring them unto the place that I have chosen to set my name there." (Neh. 1:9.) Gracious promise! It challenges the appropriation of every captive child. All who, like the penitent captives, yield with all their hearts, will hear a voice divinely sweet, whispering: "I will heal their backslidings, I will love them freely; for mine anger is turned away from him."

With the returning captives sorrow was turned into shouts and songs of victory. "And they sang together, by course in praising and giving thanks unto the Lord; because he is good, for his mercy endureth forever towards Israel. And all the people shouted with a great shout when they praised the Lord, because the foundation of the house of the Lord was laid." How like the songs of joy and gladness and shouts of holy triumph that burst from the lips of souls amid the blessed victories in spiritual Canaan regained!

After years that seemed ages of soul-bondage, how inexpressibly blessed to be again in the glorious experience indicated by the prophet when he said, "Therefore they shall come and sing in the height of Zion, and shall flow together for the goodness of the Lord, for the wheat, and for the wine and for the oil, and for the young of the flock and of the herd; and their soul shall be as a watered garden, and they shall not sorrow any more at all. For I will turn their mourning into joy, and will comfort them, and make them rejoice from their sorrow."

Back from Babylon! Soul-bondage, darkness, and spiritual woe forever left behind! The deep, deep pit of the backslider escaped before it was eternally too late! What wonder that hallelujahs of thanksgiving freely arise towards heaven? Back to Canaan; into liberty, light, and happiness; from the pit of hell to the antechamber of heaven! For such a deliverance, "glory be to God in the highest" for evermore!

Behold, happy is the man whom God correcteth; therefore despise not thou the chastening of the Almighty: for he maketh sore and bindeth up: he woundeth and his hands make whole. He shall deliver thee in six troubles: yea, in seven there shall no evil touch thee. In famine he shall redeem thee from death: and in war from the power of the sword. Thou shalt be hid from the scourge of the tongue: neither shalt thou be afraid of destruction when it cometh. At destruction and famine thou shalt laugh: neither shalt thou be afraid of the beasts of the earth. For thou shalt be in league with the stones of the field: and the beasts of the field shall be at peace with thee. And thou shalt know that thy tabernacle shall be in peace; and thou shalt visit thy habitation and shalt not sin. Thou shalt know also that thy seed shall be great, and thine offspring as the grass of the earth. Thou shalt come to thy grave in a full age, like as a shock of corn cometh in in its season. (Bible)

12

Out of Canaan into Heaven

Prelude

AND IT CAME TO pass, as they still went on, and talked, that, behold, there appeared a chariot of fire, and horses of fire, and parted them both asunder; and Elijah went up by a whirlwind into heaven. — 2 Kings 2:11.

And Stephen, being full of the Holy Ghost, looked up steadfastly into heaven, and saw the glory of God, and Jesus standing on the right hand of God. And said, Behold, I see the heavens opened and Jesus standing on the right hand of God. —Acts 8:55, 56.

> *To those who dwell in Beulah land*
> > *The heavenly kingdom's close "at hand,"*
> *For heaven's King, with empire sweet,*
> > *Is crowned within, his reign complete.*
> *And whether here, or whether there,*
> > *If reigning with him, who does care?*
> *"To live is Christ, to die is gain:"*
> > *In either case we'll not complain.*
> *'Tis joy to live, 'tis joy to die,*
> > *And will be evermore on high.*
> *As up we fly on wings of light,*
> > *We'll praise our King in mansions bright.*

Out of Canaan into Heaven

ONE AFTER ANOTHER THE faithful in the earthly Canaan came to the banks of death's river and triumphantly braved its terrors, and were borne to their everlasting home on high. Joshua, Samuel, Josiah, Elijah, Elisha, Isaiah, Jeremiah, Ezekiel, and throngs of faithful "fathers and mothers" in Israel, and young men and maidens called in life's morning, and precious little ones, joined their kindred in the heavenly paradise.

As their Canaan proved the antechamber of heaven, so, faithful, will ours. They went singly; so must we.

> *Not pressing through the portals*
> *Of the celestial town,*
> *An army of fresh immortals*
> *By the Lord of Battles won;*
> *But one by one we come*
> *To the Gate of the Heavenly Home.*
>
> —B. M.

They were singly presented with heavenly raiment, and doubtless we likewise shall be.

> *That all the powers of heaven*
> *May shout aloud to God,*
> *As each new robe of life is given,*
> *Bought by the Master's blood;*
> *And the heavenly raptures dawn*
> *On the Pilgrims, one by one.*
>
> —B. M.

Doubtless they were individually welcomed by the Father, and like honor awaits all who are promoted from spiritual Canaan.

> *That to each the voice of the Father*
> *May thrill in welcome sweet,*
> *And round each the angels gather*
> *With songs on the shining street,*
> *As one by one we go*
> *To the glory none may know.*
>
> —B. M.

Such greetings, were there no further glories to be unfolded, would repay an hundredfold Joshua for "following fully," Jeremiah for his "imprisonment," Daniel for his night in the "lions' den," and the numberless sufferers, whose names are not recorded, who were "tortured not accepting deliverance," who had "trial of cruel mockings and scourgings, yea, moreover, of bonds and imprisonment," who were "stoned," "sawn asunder," "tempted," and "slain with the sword."

To abide in spiritual Canaan is to make such welcomes as sure as existence. In passing from spiritual Canaan on earth to the heavenly Canaan *each departs differently.* "We all do fade as a leaf." Some fade early; others later. Some swiftly; others slowly. Some drop gently; others are borne by the whirlwind's blast. So with these bodies; and the same diversity marks the exit of our immortal spirits.

Some pass smilingly.

> *Have we not caught that smiling*
> *On some beloved face,*
> *As if a heavenly sound were willing*
> *The soul from our earthly place?*
> *The distant sound and sweet*
> *Of the Master's coming feet.*
>
> *We may clasp the loved one faster,*
> *And plead for a little while;*
> *But who can resist the Master?*
> *And we read, by that bright'ning smile,*
> *That the tread we may not hear*
> *Is surely drawing near.*
>
> —B. M.

Others pass unexpectedly.

> *Or in the hush of Summer weather,*
> *In the golden afternoon,*
> *As we watch by a friend's sick-bed together,*
> *And murmur, "Better soon,"*
> *Sudden the Master's feet*
> *May be heard in the sunny street!*

Till then no dream of dying
  Had flashed through the sick man's heart;
But a sudden smile on his face is lying,
  And the soul rises up to depart,
    At the sound of those gentle feet,
    Which come up through the sunny street.

—B. M.

Some pass dreamily.

Or perchance he lieth sleeping,
  With weary hand and head;
And does not hear our weeping,
  Nor the sound of that solemn tread,
    Telling the hour is come
    For his returning home.

Then, trying to still our weeping,
  With trembling lips we say,
'We must break on this silent sleeping,
  We must prepare his way.'
    And we stoop to murmur low,
    'Are you ready, dear, to go?

The Master is come, and calleth
  For thee; he is at the door.
Awake! for his shadow falleth
  Already across the floor.
    Are you ready, dear, to go
    With him that loveth so?'

And gently enters the Master;
  Through the room his garments sweep;
And our trembling hearts beat faster,
  And our eyes forget to weep
    Though we can hear him say,
    Thou shalt be THERE today.'

—B. M.

Others pass unexpectedly.

> *Behold as we kneel down trembling,*
> *The thunder crasheth free;*
> *The door bursts open wildly,*
> *And, startled, we rise to see—*
> *Serene and still and fair—*
> *The Master standing there!*
>
> *He looketh upon us sweetly,*
> *With his well-known greeting, 'Peace!'*
> *And he fills our hearts completely,*
> *And the sounds of the tempests cease.*
> *But we know that the hour is come*
> *For one of us to go home.*
>
> —B. M.

Some pass, administering consolation to loved ones left behind. Language like that which the poet puts in the mouth of the young wife of Ezekiel as she was heeding the heavenly call, flows freely from their lips.

> *Suffer me to go*
> *To Him that calleth me! I love thee so*
> *That none but he could woo me from thy side,*
> *Or make my heart content to go from thee*
> *To all the joys of heaven. And from the walls*
> *Of that bright Palace-Home my soul will lean*
> *At morn and eve, to catch some distant sound*
> *Of thy homecoming feet—as here I watched*
> *For thy return at eve.*
> *If God had willed,*
> *I would have gladly stayed; but we are his,*
> *And it is sweet to do a little thing*
> *For him that loves us so.*
>
> —B. M.

As his children pass from Canaan below to heaven above, God the Father "watches" them.

> Day and night God standeth,
> Scanneth each soul as it landeth,
>   Watching the dim, sweet smile
> That shines in the shadowy place
> On many a death-washed face;
>   Watching to see the victor light
> In his children's eyes as they struggle free
> From the waves of their dread death agony!
>
> —B. M.

Christ, their Saviour, sympathizes with them.

> Day and night Christ standeth,
> Scanning each soul as it landeth;
> Over the floods he bendeth,
>   With a face that hath been dead;
> With a mouth that once did cry,
> From these waves in agony,
>   'The waters go over my head!'
>
> —B. M.

He meets and upholds them.

> And when his children rise,
> To pass through the dreary river,
> To the shore they had not trod,
> Unto the face of God,
> Though their eyes grow blind with death,
> And they stumble in the stream
> As men in a deadly dream,
> Christ stretcheth forth his hand
> A gentle, pierced hand
> And draws them safe to land.
>
> —B. M.

Some depart amid the visions of the heavenly world.

> *For some, like dying Stephen,*
>   *The city bright behold;*
> *And view its walls of jasper,*
>   *Its streets of shining gold.*
>   *They triumph over every fear,*
>   *And smile to see their home so near.*

> *The King in all his glory*
>   *They see in vision bright;*
> *With angel hosts and loved ones,*
>   *All clad in robes of light.*
>   *The glory of the realms divine,*
>   *Reflected, makes their faces shine.*

> *They see, down countless vistas*
>   *Of cycles yet to be,*
> *The glory that awaiteth*
>   *Throughout eternity.*
>   *And weaned from earth by scenes like this,*
>   *They gladly rise to realms of bliss.*

They pass from spiritual Canaan to heaven triumphantly.

> *With joy and holy triumph,*
>   *The glad soul breaks its chain,*
> *And soars with hallelujahs,*
>   *To join the heavenly train;*
>   *And "floating" high in realms of light,*
>   *It quickly passes from our sight.*

> *Or like the sainted Cookman,*
>   *Washed in the Savior's blood,*
> *With raiment pure and spotless,*
>   *They praise the Triune God.*

And "sweeping" through the pearly gate,
Thus pass to their eternal state.

Or 'mid the acclamations
Of shining hosts on high,
They rise, like grand Elijah,
In triumph through the sky.
The King himself their royal guide,
Triumphantly to heaven they ride.

Their promotion from the spiritual on earth to the heavenly Canaan, though sad to loved ones left behind, yet is precious to their Savior. It is written, "Precious in the sight of the Lord is the death of his saints."

We grieve and yield to sadness,
When saints leave earthly employ;
But thrilled with holy gladness,
They rise on wings of joy.
Their Savior calls to realms of light,
Their "death is precious" in his sight.

Their sorrows now are ended,
Their trials all are o'er;
Their lives with his are blended
As one, for evermore.
Their Savior calls to realms of light,
Their "death is precious" in his sight.

Their songs and glad employments
Are changed for those above,
Where new and rich enjoyments
Bespeak their Father's love.
Their Savior calls to realms of light,
Their "death is precious" in his sight.

Their prison bars are broken;
Above its bolts they rise;
The welcome word is spoken,
That bids them to the skies.
Their Savior calls to realms of light,
Their "death is precious" in his sight.

And now amid the splendors
Of that eternal home,
They claim through Christ their mansion,
And sit upon his throne.
Their Savior calls to realms of light,
Their "death is precious" in his sight.

In heaven above "they rest from their labors, and their works do follow them."

Their rest on earth was very sweet,
And yet could be but incomplete;
For while their souls were then at rest,
Their bodies oft were much oppressed.

At home, abroad, on land and sea,
They toiled and suffered patiently.
Their Master did, and why not they,
With gladness, walk the toilsome way?

For Jesus' sake, by men reviled,
They "fools" and "lunatics" were styled;
By formalists were coldly spurned,
And often at the stake were burned.

Because for Christ they stood alone,
They sometimes to the beasts were thrown;
Were beaten, stoned, and crucified;
Or, starved in dungeons dark, they died.

But see! their souls exultant soar
To rest with Christ for evermore.
He greets them with a sweet "Well done,"
And leads them to their restful home.

When toiling here their joy was great;
Who now their raptures can relate?
They humbly fall at Jesus' feet,
And praise him for their rest so sweet.

Then, clad with strength that he has given,
They rise to do his will in heaven,
Where service tireless shall be,
Though lasting through eternity.

While there on errands glad they go,
"Their works" are sweeping on below;
The seed they scattered far and wide
Has swiftly grown and multiplied.

And nurtured by the blood they gave,
Behold a ripening harvest wave!
No sights in heaven can give them bliss,
Nor rapture raise so much as this.

As one by one the stars appear
When evening shades are drawing near,
Till mighty constellations rise
And glorify the evening skies,

Just so, the saints that labored here
Shall see their "works" above appear,
As one by one their souls arise,
To brighten the celestial skies.

Let earth and heaven forever ring,
  And the Savior's praises sing;
By every tongue may he be blest,
  Who grants his people such a rest!

All who pass from spiritual Canaan into heaven shall be esteemed unspeakably precious in their Savior's sight. "They shall be a *crown of glory* in the hand of the Lord, and a *royal diadem* in the hand of thy God." "For they shall be as the stones of a crown, lifted up as an ensign upon his land." "And they shall be mine, saith the Lord of hosts, in that day when I make up my jewels. (Bible)

Shining for the Master,
  "Crowns" of wondrous worth,
Rescued from disaster,
  'Mid the mines of earth.
"In his hand" triumphant,
  Evermore to be
Worn o'er all victorious,
  Through eternity.

"Diadems" of splendor,
  Shining, pure and bright;
Gleaming on forever
  With increasing light;
Royally exalted
  By the King above;
Monuments of mercy,
  Wonders of his love.

"Diadems" so precious!
  Bought by blood divine,
In the highest heavens
  Evermore to shine.
O, what wondrous beauty!
  O, what matchless worth!

Can it be that ever
  They belonged to earth?

"Jewels" from the ocean,
  Hidden long from sight,
Till the Master sought them,
  Found, and brought to light;
Rescued from the billows
  By his wondrous grace;
Bore in holy triumph
  To his royal place.

Now, o'er all victorious,
  As the angels bow,
See his "crown of jewels"
  Placed on Jesus' brow!
Wonderful salvation!
  Love beyond degree!
Glorious exaltation!
  Grand eternity!

  In heaven we shall still continue to exert an influence on earth. "He, being dead, yet speaketh."

Still speaking! through the hours,
  Or ages that have flown,
Since first 'twas sadly whispered
  In accents low, "He's gone."
    Whence come those voices clear and strong,
    That cheer our waiting hearts so long?

Still speaking? deeds of kindness,
  And acts of charity,
Which men in human blindness
  Were slow at first to see,
    Now speak in tones so sweet and clear
    That friend and foe alike must hear.

Still speaking! souls enlightened
  And saved through them while here,
The whole wide world have brightened
  With words and deeds of cheer.
    Through these they speak from year to year
    In tones that grow more strong and clear.

Still speaking! How their presence,
  Like sweet and heavenly lyres,
Dispelling grief and sadness,
  With holy joy inspires!
    They come so near, and seem so real,
    Their presence we can often feel.

Still speaking! Warning voices,
  Of man's mortality,
And need of preparation
  To meet Eternity!
    In solemn tones their accents roll
    Through all the chambers of the soul.

Still speaking! Winning accents
  Of peace, and joy, and love,
Of mansions bright and heavenly,
  In kingly courts above,
    These tones with fondest memories fill,
    And all our hearts with rapture thrill.

Still speaking! Tender accents,
  To those who loved them best,
The little band and faithful,
  More precious than the rest:
    To these they speak in tones so dear
    That other listeners must not hear.
Still speaking! Anguished voices
  Like Christ's on Calvary,

That tell of pain and suffering,
  To save humanity
    In tones of agony they plead
    That we for souls should intercede.

Still speaking! Triumphing voices,
  Like Jesus' when he rose,
And, rising, conquered Death itself
  And routed all his foes.
    These tones of victory banish fear,
    And speak of final triumph near.

Still speaking! Abel speaketh,
  And Moses, John, and Paul,
And Luther, Huss, and Wesley,
  Still speak to one and all;
    Yea, every saint who faithful dies,
    Still speaks for Jesus from the skies.

Still speaking! As the shower
  Still speaks, though passed away,
By brightening leaf and flower
  For many a coming day,
    So speak the fully sanctified
    Who, cleansed from sin, have crossed the tide.

Still speaking! Ceaseless voices!
  Speak on from shore to shore,
And let your sacred accents
  Be heard for evermore!
    How sweet the portion of the blest,
    To speak like this from realms of rest.

Those who are *promoted from spiritual Canaan to heavenly shores above*, enter upon a career marvelous beyond conception. "Let them that love him be as the sun when he *goeth forth in his might*." "Then shall the

righteous shine forth as the *sun* in the kingdom of their Father." (Bible)
Some of the following features with force apply to the "saints" below as
well as above:

> *Freely, gladly shining,*
> *   Like the sun above,*
> *Glow the saints of Jesus*
> *   With the fire of love;*
>
> *Grandly, clearly beaming*
> *   In eternal youth,*
> *Shedding forth forever*
> *   Blessed light of Truth.*
>
> *Ever treading onward*
> *   In their orbits bright,*
> *Like the sun above us,*
> *   Move the saints of light.*
>
> *Mighty systems centers*
> *   In the world of bliss;*
> *Move the saints in glory,*
> *   As the sun in this;*
>
> *Shining without effort,*
> *   Fed by God alone,*
> *Like the sun above us,*
> *   Circling round his throne.*
>
> *Shedding life and beauty*
> *   On their gladsome way*
> *Banishers of darkness,*
> *   Like the King of Day;*
>
> *Guided in their motions*
> *   By the hand divine,*

Like the sun, in glory
  Evermore they shine.

When the mighty fires
  Of the sun shall cease,
Still more mighty, theirs
  Ever shall increase.

Glory, hallelujah!
  To the Lamb divine!
What a glorious prospect,
  Thus in bliss to shine!

13

Canaan Contrasts and Inquiries

Prelude

If we open wide our eyes,
  Earth and ocean, clouds and skies,
All things visible, will show
  Lessons that we need to know.
Object lessons they will be,
  Helping us the truth to see.
Teacher, help us so to learn
  That within thy love will burn
With a pure and brightening flame,
  That shall glorify thy name.

Canaan Contrasts and Inquiries

PEOPLE IN SPIRITUAL EGYPT are like an engine headed the wrong way and "ditched." In the "Sinai Wilderness of Justification they are like the same engine redeemed from the ditch, on the track, headed the right way, attached to a train; but somewhat rusty, and making slow progress because of lack of steampower. In the "Desert Wilderness" they are like the murderous engine which has shot from the track, and carried with it a train of cars, and is buried beneath its wreck and the mangled bodies of those whom it has ruined. In Canaan they are like the engine, brightly burnished, completely equipped, moving at full speed, and gaily bearing its ponderous load as if it were a feather. In spiritual Babylon they are like an express engine, which, moving heavily laden with passengers, at its utmost speed, has plunged with them from the track down an awful precipice. Their condition is worse than those in the "Desert Wilderness," because they have fallen further.

Reader, what kind of an engine are you? "Ditched," "rusty and steamless," "wrecked," or "burnished and completely equipped?"

Egypt is spiritual Winter; justification, spiritual Spring; backsliding, spiritual Winter, with constant blizzards and the thermometer sixty degrees below zero. Canaan is spiritual Summer; maturity in Canaan, spiritual Autumn; heaven, the spiritual garner; hell, the spiritual "chaff heap."

Where art thou? All who persist in staying in spiritual Egypt are like children who "won't go to school," but pass their time on the street. In the Sinai Wilderness experience they are like children in the primary department who have enrolled their names and are trying to gain an education. In the Desert Wilderness they are like children who, disobeying both parents and teacher, play "truant" and squander the time in some foolish way. In Babylon they are like "truants" in jail. In spiritual Canaan they are like pupils who not only are in school, but love both to be there and to study; have passed the primary department, and in the higher grades are making cheerful and rapid progress. Those who are "mature" in spiritual Canaan are like students engaged in the university course.

Heaven above to the saint is beginning life-work after graduating in these spiritual courses below. Hell is the punishing place of refractory pupils, and those who "would not go to school."

Have you entered "Jesus' school?" If so, in what department are you? Are you a "primary" Christian? a "higher grade" Christian? It may be that, by God's grace, you are in the "university course," and, after a little more discipline below, you will be called upon to begin your life-work above!

God forbid that we should be "truant" "jailed," or remain all our days in the primary department, lest it shall be said of us as of spiritual dunces of other days, "Ye are dull of hearing; for when for the time ye ought to be teachers, ye have need that one teach you again what be the first principles of the oracles of God."

Spiritual Egypt is like a poisonous, swampy spring, filthy, and easy of access, but whose waters bring certain death. The "Sinai Wilderness" state is like a surface well-water good, but pump poor. Spiritual Canaan is like the bedrock artesian well, whose pure, cold waters flow spontaneously the year round. Babylon is a well without water, full of poisonous gas. Maturity in Canaan is like the artesian well, with pipes so arranged as to carry the water wherever needed.

What kind of water are you drinking? Poisoned or pure; surface or bedrock?

When quite young, we had an old checked pump, that often had to be primed before it would work. It usually took both my brother and myself to work it. One would pour in the water, and the other would, with might, work the handle; and after much ado, water would be secured. Some professors are just like that old pump: their religious life is "checked" in a good many places; they always have to be "primed" before they will work, and then it takes two men to get from them the work of one. Would you not rather be an "artesian well" Christian, continually fed yourself by the great Fountain of Living Waters, and doing Christian duty gladly and spontaneously, with pipes so adjusted that you will bear the water of life wherever the Master wills?

Egypt is spiritual night; justification, spiritual twilight and cloudy weather. "Wandering" is spiritual night, attended by constant cyclones and earthquakes. Canaan is spiritual sunshine. Maturity in Canaan is spiritual noontide. Heaven above is celestial day, where they have no need of the sun, neither of the moon to shine in it; "for the glory of God" and "the Lamb" are the light thereof.

Heavenly Father, help each reader to just now clearly comprehend whether with them it is "night," or "twilight," or "cloudy," or "stormy earthquake, darkness," or "sunrise," or "noontide!"

To be in spiritual Egypt is to be in rebellion against God. To be in the "Sinai Wilderness" state is to have "surrendered," taken the "oath of allegiance" to God, received "pardon" and citizenship. To be in the "Desert Wilderness" is to have "deserted" God's army and have joined the enemy. To be in spiritual Canaan is to so love God and his government as to *gladly* do anything or go anywhere that their interests may demand. It is to have every rebellious impulse cleansed away, and a spirit of pure devotion to the divine commonwealth. To be a "mature" Christian is to have had experience in Canaan service for our King. Heaven is "the soldiers' home;" the judgment day their "grand review."

Are you a "rebel," or have you received "pardon" and "citizenship?" Have you been guilty of imperiling God's government by "sleeping on your post?" Are you a "deserter?" I trust that you are a true and pure "soldier" of the cross; more heroic and self-sacrificing for your God than ever patriot was for his nation.

To be in Egypt is to be like a tree that bears poisonous fruit. To be justified is to be like one that is alive, and yields some good fruit. To be a backslider is to be like a tree that is "dead." To be in spiritual Babylon is to be like a tree that is "twice dead, plucked up by the roots." To be in spiritual Canaan is to be like "a tree planted by the rivers of water, that bringeth forth his fruit in his season; his leaf also shall not wither; and whatsoever he doeth shall prosper."

Reader, what kind of a tree are you? Are you a poisonous tree? Are you "fruitless?" Are you "dead?" Are you "twice dead?" Or, are you the "fruitful" tree planted by the rivers of water?

In Egypt the "language of Canaan" is unknown. The justified believer is master of its alphabet, and can speak some words. "In the land" it comes just as natural as the "other tongues" at the day of Pentecost. How far have you advanced? A conceited young man was boasting that he was master of the French, Spanish, Portuguese, and Italian languages. "Now and then he uttered an oath, declaring that he knew almost all languages!" He was stopped by an elderly listener, "asking him if he were at all acquainted with the 'language of Canaan.' " May we be wise enough not to boast of our learning until we have mastered that! Then we will be beyond boasting.

Do you see that black drop of water in the center of that stagnant pool? A few hours have passed, and now it is morning, and that black drop has been transformed into a crystal dew-drop, and is suspended from a beautiful rosebud. It is now the early dawning — and listen! It whispers to its sister-drops, and is speaking of the sun. It says, "I've heard that the sun can 'fill' a dew-drop 'full' of light and warmth; but that seems to me to be a very high state of dew-drop grace, and I can't believe that he could 'fill' me; and if he did, I fear I could not be kept full."

Older and wiser drops smiled at the emphasis that their sister put upon the word "*me*," and at the idea that the mighty sun could not purify and beautify a little dew-drop without crippling his resources, and blinked in the twilight as they awaited his welcome rays. See! His beams now gild the clouds, now the hills; and now they fall upon the little dew-drop that, humbled by her sisters' words, had decided to warmly welcome them. See how it dances with holy joy, as, made all radiant by the sunlight, it glistens like a diamond! And is the sun exhausted? Listen as he laughs at the little drop, and majestically moves on with power to fill and thrill infinite millions of dew-drops like it. But did you see? The little drop glistened in its appointed place until its Maker said, ' It is enough; come up higher." Then it kissed the rosebud goodbye, took its seat triumphantly in a chariot of golden sunlight, and, "floating in light," it rose higher and higher, until by and by it greeted millions of kindred drops that had gone before it; and now, with them, we see it glorified, far, far above the earth, with all the tints of the rainbow.

The black drop in the stagnant pool is like the sinner in spiritual Egypt. The hesitating dew-drop, hanging in the twilight, craving yet hesitating to claim the radiant baptism, is like the justified believer. The drop, filled with the cleansing, illuminating, warming baptism from above, is like the believer in spiritual Canaan, under the like baptism of the Holy Spirit. In its heavenward ascent, glorification and mingling with kindred drops above, it is like the saint, when, like Elijah, he triumphantly enters his chariot and ascends to the home of the glorified.

May we each be as yielding to the influences of the "SUN of righteousness" as the drop was to the influences of the "sun of day." Then speedily, like it, will we be drawn from Egypt's stagnant pools to blissful realms on earth, and then to brighter worlds above, where forever we will sing and shout glad hosannas that we, by divine grace, were led "Out of Egypt Into Canaan."

Reader, if you do thus "yield yourself unto God," will you not, before you lay aside this book, sign and, by God's assisting grace, ever keep the following "Canaan Covenant;" and then seek to win as many others as you can to cross with you the "Jordan," enter the "land," and with you evermore abide there?

Canaan Covenant

Heavenly Father, by thy assisting grace, "all that thou commandest us we will do; and whithersoever thou sendest us we will go." We believe that thou dost lead us into spiritual Canaan, and we promise to trust thee ever to keep us therein.

NAMES   DATE

_____   _____

_____   _____

14

From Egyptian Bondage to Canaan Liberty

Prelude

> *What we have felt and seen,*
> *With confidence we tell,*
> *And publish to the sons of men*
> *The signs infallible.*

Personal Experience of the Author

MY ONLY OBJECT IN relating this is to glorify God. I love to tell what he has done for me, and in this way can do so, not only while I live and where I am, but where I may not be able to personally go, and after I have gone to heaven above.

God gave me an earnest Christian mother, and, through her influence, made precious impressions upon me when young, that never were totally erased. I cannot remember when I did not think of God and of eternity. My *Egypt* experiences lasted from the time I reached years of accountability until I was nineteen. Sometimes my heart was tender; but it grew harder as the years advanced. Awful conviction would sometimes possess me, but I quenched it. I grew very giddy. I came to dislike meetings, preachers, and all religious society. I would go without my meals rather than enter the house when a minister was there, and threatened to leave home if mother mentioned eternal matters. Thus sadly Satan blinded me.

Mother would sometimes lay the Testament where I could not help seeing it when retiring, with some passage marked for me to read. Repeatedly I dreamed the day of judgment had come, earth was burning, the Judge descending, and *I* unprepared!

> *For years I bore about hell in my breast;*
> *When I thought of my God it was nothing but gloom;*

> *Day brought me no pleasure, night gave me no rest,*
> *There was still the grim shadow of horrible doom.*

Egyptian night grew blacker and, duped by my spiritual Pharaoh, I tried to be an infidel. God's grace, through mother's prayers, prevented. In hundreds of ways my Savior tried to win me from my servitude of sin; but, deluded by the enemy, I would not be won. When seventeen, through mother's plans and sacrifice, I began my studies at Albion. Here I met her who is now my wife. She was a genuine Christian, and, next to mother, became instrumental in my conversion. In my Egyptian experience mother was my Moses, and she my Aaron. The sepulchral tones and sanctimonious ways of some professors had set me against their kind of religion; but I was saved from being mystified by my Moses and Aaron, in whom the blessed, soul-cheering, joy-bringing gospel shone in all its purity.

Death scenes and funeral processions were a terror to me. The Spirit often used them to mightily arrest me. The following words haunted me like echoes from a graveyard:

> *Come, ye young, ye merry, proud,*
> *You must die and wear a shroud;*
> *Time will rob you of your bloom,*
> *Death will drag you to the tomb;*
> *Then you'll cry, 'Woe unto me!*
> *Lost, through all eternity!'*

O, how can I be thankful enough that I was not then cut off!

> *Yes! death would have come and its angel have torn me*
> *By force, to the judgment where hope could not be,*
> *And the spirit of darkness from thence would have borne me*
> *To unspeakable woes in his wide, burning sea.*

> *Where the worms, and the wails, and the lashes cease never,*
> *My poor ruined soul would have sickened of fire,*
> *And I should be tortured forever and ever;*
> *But the pains of eternity never would tire.*

I became fully convinced of my lost condition, yet would own it to none but my "Aaron." I was irritable when approached on the subject by any other. She believed that it was wrong for Christians to be "unequally yoked together with unbelievers," and her loyalty to God led her to say, "I never can marry an unconverted man." She kindly yet persistently urged an immediate and complete surrender to God. I was brought face to face with God and duty, and knew that I ought to yield.

The tempter said, "There is time enough yet;" and for a time I listened to his voice and was supremely miserable. Day and night thoughts of God, judgment, and eternal doom conspired to make me wretched. I resolved to yield. Then whispered the tempter: "Be a silent Christian." I tried it. I began to read my Bible, kneel at the family altar, where in my pride of heart I had for a long time sat upright, and in silence try to pray. I felt that these were steps in the right direction, but got no peace. Thus for some time I tried to compromise matters with God and bring him to my terms, but he would not come.

Hitherto God had gently entreated me by his servants. At this point I was made to feel that trifling with God in this halfhearted way must cease or he would come with sterner measures. I did not heed the warning, and then his judgment fell with crushing weight upon my soul. O, the horrors of those days of darkness! I had been forewarned, and knew I deserved all; so I could not murmur. Alone in the woods again, I sought to settle the question. I fell upon my knees and tried to pray. The question came: "Will you now fully yield?"

I said, "In all things but just that one — I cannot open my school with prayer." This was my Red Sea.

I could get no peace, and whenever I tried to pray that question would rise like a specter before me. I would say, "Anything but that;" but it was God's test question and he would not be turned away. At this point the impression came, *"Now or never! Yield at once, or you will suddenly be cut off and forever lost!"* This came like a lightning stroke. I felt as sure of its truth as that I lived. The next Monday morning my school began. Tremblingly I took my Bible and read one of the shortest Psalms I could find, and then my courage failed me. The next, and the next morning the same was repeated.

Thursday morning I said, "This will do no longer. I will fully obey." God helped, and I did as best I could, and then it was O, so easy to fully trust! And before the sun went down that night the witness of the Spirit was given, and peace-sweet, deep, rich, and inexpressible—was mine. My warfare with God was ended, past sins were all forgiven, the power of sin was broken, the first letter in the alphabet of redemption was learned, and I began the new life.

I wrote at once to my friends of the change, made a public profession at the first opportunity, was baptized, and united with the Church. Soon came my call to the ministry and preparation for that work. When twenty-three we married, and since then have gladly labored to bring others to Him who sought and saved us.

Fourteen years have passed since I crossed the Red Sea, and I have never for a moment felt like returning to Egyptian bondage. Glory to God in the highest for such wonderful deliverance!

For nine years I tarried in the Sinai Wilderness experience. I was converted, and knew it, loved God and his people, worked for him as well as I could, saw many souls converted, and grew in knowledge and experience; but my *temper*, which was quick, often made me conscious that I was not possessed of all the mind of Christ. I was hampered by selfish ambitions, joking and teasing tendencies, and other movements of the carnal mind. Inbred sin sought to expel the holy power that bound it, and there were frequent struggles within between the two contending principles. I needed the blessing mentioned in the following song prayer of a well-known poet:

> *Savior of the sin-sick soul,*
> *Give me grace to make me whole;*
> *Finish thy great work of grace;*
> *Cut it short in righteousness.*
>
> *Speak the second time, 'Be clean;'*
> *Take away my inbred sin;*
> *Every stumbling block remove;*
> *Cast it out by perfect love.*

I had read much on the subject of heart purity, but never heard a sermon on it. I knew that the Bible clearly taught cleansing from inbred sin, and the fullness of the Spirit as the privilege of every believer. I reasoned: "God does not do things by halves. I know that he converted me and that I am his child, therefore I must be saved from inbred sin." The fact, however, that it was in my heart, and that I often was painfully conscious of it, was stronger than my argument and confused me. I said, "I'll keep it down;" but instead of that it kept me down. Then I said, "It must be a growth; I'll grow into it." I did grow in the knowledge of self and Christian privilege, but made little progress in the grace of perfect love. How it pains me that in my dullness I tarried so long in shallow waters when the great deep of God's love was continually inviting!

In November, 1882, I permitted the Lord to lead me to Kadesh Barnea, on the borders of the promised land. By his grace I then and there entered the land, receiving the blessed baptism of the Spirit that cleanses from inbred sin, and fills with perfect love. In June I had appointed a three day's special service for myself and people to seek this longed-for experience. Rev. William Taylor and wife, two noble workers who had the fullness of the Spirit, were invited to assist. It was a time of deep heart-searching. Their testimonies and teachings were clear and given in all humility, and convinced me all the deeper of my great need and privilege. I received great help at that time, but not the consciousness that the great work was wrought.

In November the crisis came. I had been preaching full salvation, but could lead my people no further than I had gone myself. I set apart a time to settle the matter. God met me and gave me the promise, "If we walk in the light as he is in the light, we have fellowship one with another, and the blood of Jesus Christ his Son *cleanseth* us from *all* sin."

The blessed Holy Spirit explained it to my heart, and helped me to take hold of it right *then* and *there*. He suggested: "Why not believe *on the authority of his Word* that God is doing just what he agrees to do *just now?*" I was conscious that the conditions upon which the promise was based were being met, and could see no reason why I should not, and replied: "Lord, I do." In an instant I was made conscious of my cleansing. The "giants" fled, the "walled towns" crumbled, and Canaan, through Christ, was possessed. To God be all the glory!

The "fullness" soon followed. I saw then where my trouble had been. I had not dared to venture on the promise and *trust in the present tense*. I thanked God for the victory given, and asked that, in order with greater confidence I might publicly proclaim and urge the experience, that he would give me still further unmistakable evidence of its reality. I retired, looking for something more.

I was not disappointed. Instead of some*thing*, some*one* came — the *One* altogether lovely, even Christ himself. I had slept about an hour when I was suddenly awakened by what sounded like three distinct knocks on the front door. In an instant I was made just as conscious of the Divine Presence as ever man was of the company of an earthly friend. I felt the presence of a gentle, unseen power upon my head. Then a wave of divine power and love, causing a sensation something like an electric shock, only inexpressibly pleasurable, rolled over my entire being. Then three impressions were made just as vividly as if uttered by an audible voice:

1. "This is the added evidence you prayed for."
2. "You are healed of your disease."
3. "A definite call to especial evangelistic work."

A few days after, my wife received a call to the same work. Since then, without the break of an hour, both the blessing and the *Blesser* have been mine.

For years I had been suffering from the effects of a sunstroke. It had taken me from my studies, and threatened to prostrate me completely. Every year of my preaching, some had thought, would be my last. Physicians said my only hope was to stop and rest. The physical cure wrought was perfect. Both the spiritual and physical blessings stand the test of toil and time. Great and gratifying as the physical healing is, I count it a mere shadow compared with the spiritual uplift then received. My wife says I have been a changed man. My members said there was a marked improvement in my preaching. Teasing, foolish jesting, and selfishness, by the Divine Plowman were rooted out, and the Spirit's graces implanted in their stead. The second letter in redemption's alphabet has been learned, and a holy ambition aspires to further progress, and then to teach to those unlearned.

Nearly five years have passed since Christ took complete possession of my soul. *He abides.* At first, for an instant, I would sometimes let go of him; but he has taught me to constantly and obediently trust him, and while doing so *he stays.* I have been tempted much, but he has given victory. I find a deepening love for him and for his Church below.

The impression made upon my mind to engage in evangelistic work continued to deepen. I said, "If this be of God, I will receive a call from the Church to engage in it." I soon found, however, that our beloved Church does not yet officially recognize this office, and hence has no appointed agencies to call to this work. I found that the work was Scriptural, and that the Holy Ghost, in this and other generations, had in a marvelous manner set his seal upon it.

Then came invitation after invitation from the brethren to assist them in the very work to which we felt God was calling us. To some of these we were able to respond, and both on our own charge and in these places souls were converted and believers sanctified.

Thus we reached a point where the Spirit's voice, the call of the Church through the many invitations to the work, fruitage in the work, and the open door, all combined to convince us that the call was from God. I therefore at our Michigan conference asked to be set free for this work. The conference granted the request, and by passing the following, further gave its sanction and set its seal upon the act:

> Whereas, our brother, M. W. Knapp, has taken a certificate of location, in order to engage in evangelistic work; and
>
> Whereas, We believe that the Holy Spirit has led him to this step; therefore, be it
>
> *Resolved*, That we shall be glad to re-admit Brother Knapp at any time when the way shall open for his return to us; that, knowing the gifts, graces, and usefulness of Brother Knapp and his wife, we do cordially commend them to the fellowship and co-operation of God's people everywhere, and to the blessings of God in their work.

Pastoral work, which often was distasteful before entering Canaan, has proved delightful since. Preaching and other soul-saving work is blissful beyond expression. I would rather be an evangel of the glad tidings to lost souls than an archangel. I would rather have a millionth part of an interest in the salvation of a soul than globes of solid gold without that. I am anxious for no grander heaven than God is giving year by year.

Dear reader, may we each be so faithful in the earthly Canaan that we may greet each other in the heavenly!

Unto Him that hath "called us out of darkness into his marvelous light" be glory and dominion for ever and ever! Amen.

Buy your books at 40% off the retail price!
**Join Schmul's Wesleyan Book Club
by calling us toll-free**

800-S$_7$P$_7$B$_2$O$_6$O$_6$K$_5$S$_7$

Put a discount Christian bookstore in your own mailbox.